Weight Watchers™ Pasta Cookbook

Wendy Veale

SIMON & SCHUSTER

LONDON·SYDNEY·NEW·YORK·TOKYO·SINGAPORE·TORONTO

First published in Great Britain by Simon & Schuster, 1995
A Paramount Communications Company

Copyright © 1995, Weight Watchers (UK) Ltd

Simon & Schuster Ltd
West Garden Place
Kendal Street
London W2 2AQ

Design: Green Moore Lowenhoff
Typesetting: Stylize
Photography: Karl Adamson
Styling: Maria Kelly
Food preparation: Cara Hobday

Weight Watchers Publications Manager: Delia Bintley
Weight Watchers Publications Assistant: Celia Whiston

A CIP catalogue record is available from the British Library

ISBN 0-671-71423-6

Printed and bound in Italy by Rotolito Lombarda S.p.A.

Pictured on the front cover: *Meatballs with Spaghetti in Sweet and
Sour Sauce (page 73) and Salmon and Pasta Bake (page 60)*

Pictured on the back cover: *Pasta Quills with Four Cheeses (page 45)*

Recipe notes:
Egg size is medium (size 3), unless otherwise stated.
Vegetables are medium-size, unless otherwise stated.
It is important to use proper measuring spoons, not cutlery, for spoon measures.
1 tablespoon = 15 ml; 1 teaspoon = 5 ml.
Dried herbs can be substituted for fresh ones, but the flavour will not always be so
good. Halve the fresh-herb quantity stated in the recipe.

Vegetarian recipes:
These symbols show which recipes are suitable for vegetarians.

$\mathcal{V}$ shows the recipe is vegetarian

($\mathcal{V}$) shows the recipe has a vegetarian option

Vegetarians should note that Quorn and egg pastas may contain non-free-range eggs.

Contents

Introduction   4

Soups   8

Light Dishes and Pasta Salads   14

Pasta Sauces   24

Pasta with Eggs and Cheese   34

Pasta with Fish   46

Pasta with Meat and Poultry   62

Index   80

Introduction

As a Lifetime Member – and in a career where I'm constantly surrounded by food – I am the first to admit that my passion for cooking tells on my waistband all too often! But, on the whole, the news is good! Fifteen years after reaching my Goal Weight, the Weight Watchers Programme has kept me in check and become second nature to me. The difference between then and now, I think, is that losing pounds and maintaining a healthy weight has never been easier. You have only to look at the influence of the Mediterranean way of eating to see how good food fits naturally into the Programme. From store-cupboard ingredients to fresh meats and vegetables, there has never been such an abundance of healthy and delicious foods to choose from. In my larder, pasta comes a close second to the ever-loyal canned tomato – and the two go hand in hand as the basis for an infinite number of recipes from soups and quick and easy pasta dishes with sauces, to bakes and gratins. Whether you're cooking a mid-week supper for one using store-cupboard ingredients, feeding a family or entertaining friends, pasta is convenient, versatile and delicious. It has become one of the world's favourite foods and – as you will enjoy discovering in the pages ahead – pasta brings even more colour, flavour and fun (and in all shapes and sizes) into cooking Weight Watchers style!

What is Pasta?

The word pasta literally means 'dough'. Most pastas are made from semolina flour which is milled from a hard wheat, rich in gluten, called durum wheat. The flour is combined with water and kneaded into dough, rolled out and extruded through a die or mould, then cut and dried. This pasta has a characteristic hard texture, firm to the bite – *al dente* – when cooked to perfection.

Some dried pastas are made with eggs – *all'uova*. This gives a slightly softer texture and a richer flavour when cooked, and is most common in northern Italy, where stuffed pastas are popular. Dried pasta – *pasta asciutto* – once produced only in the south of Italy, has a much firmer texture and tends to be made without eggs.

A Profusion of Pasta

Pasta is available in all shapes, colours and sizes. Although spaghetti is still at the top of the league, flavoured pastas are becoming increasingly popular. Look out for green – spinach-flavoured pasta; red – chilli-pepper or tomato-flavoured; black – dyed with cuttlefish or squid ink; and purple pastas coloured with beetroot. Then there are mushroom or herb-flavoured varieties, wholewheat pastas, and even chocolate, apple or spiced flavours!

Whatever you choose, always buy good-quality pasta made from durum wheat. Reputable dried pasta would be a wiser choice than a fresh pasta of doubtful origin, and coming towards its 'sell-by' date.

Dried pasta is an excellent store-cupboard ingredient and keeps almost indefinitely. Fresh pasta will keep in the refrigerator for only 3–5 days, but does freeze successfully.

Pasta – A Way of Life

As the basis of the healthy Mediterranean diet, it is not surprising that pasta fits so well into the Weight Watchers Programme. Pasta contains a mere 102 Calories per 1 oz (30 g) of dried pasta. That is just one Carbohydrate Selection into which you can toss fish, vegetables, cheese, poultry and delicious full-flavoured sauces. And as pasta is a complex carbohydrate, it sustains and releases energy over a long period of time, both filling you up and keeping your hunger pangs at bay!

Pasta Shapes and Sizes

Although I have suggested various pasta types with the recipes, you will no doubt want to substitute your own favourites at times. The texture, thickness and shape of a pasta will, to an extent, determine which type of sauce will best accompany it, but there are certainly no hard and fast rules. Generally speaking, *pasta lunga* – long thin pastas such as flat noodles, tagliatelle and spaghetti – are best eaten with clinging, creamy or tomato sauces and rich cheese sauces.

Pasta corta – short, thick pastas including macaroni, quills and tubes – are good with chunky sauces which cling to their ridges and hollows. The more delicate pasta shapes such as bows and ribbons are better suited to light sauces with no solids.

Pasta ripiena – filled pasta such as lasagne, cannelloni and large shells – is meant to be stuffed or layered with thick, rich sauces and baked au gratin.

Pasta in the Pot

There is a saying in Italy – 'spaghetti loves company'. In other words, don't leave the kitchen while the pasta is cooking!

Generally speaking, fresh pasta needs 3–4 minutes of cooking and dried pasta (depending on its shape) requires 8–10 minutes. Dried pasta *all'uova* (with egg) may take a minute or two less, and wholewheat pasta will take slightly longer.

Always refer to the instructions on the pack, but keep in mind these golden rules:

Conventional Cooking

- The secret of cooking pasta successfully is a large pan and plenty of lightly salted boiling water. Pasta increases 3 times in volume during cooking. Allow 2 pints (1.2 litres) of water to every 4 oz (120 g) of pasta.
- Tip all the pasta into boiling water – or feed in spaghetti, bending it around the pot as it softens.
- Bring the water back to a fast boil and stir the pasta occasionally with a wooden fork. Check the required cooking time on the manufacturer's pack.
- Have a colander and warm serving bowl ready – and your sauce cooked and ready to stir in.
- Towards the end of the cooking time, test the pasta. It should be firm and provide resistance or 'bite' – *al dente*.
- Drain the pasta, shaking the colander, and quickly turn it into a warm serving dish to take to the table *pronto!*
- Undercook pasta which is to be used in baked dishes so that it remains hard in the centre.
- When cooking pasta for a salad, rinse it with cold running water to cool it quickly and stop it from cooking further.

Microwave Cooking

Microwaving pasta is no quicker than the conventional method although it does allow you to leave the kitchen while it cooks as it is less likely to boil over. The results are good, but if you are cooking 12 oz (360 g) or more you are best reverting to a large pan on the hob!

- Use a deep, large container.
- Pour boiling water over the pasta, to cover.
- Stir well, cover with a vented lid and cook on HIGH (100%) for 3 minutes for fresh pasta or 7–8 minutes for dried.
- Allow the pasta to stand for 2–3 minutes before draining.

Types of Pasta

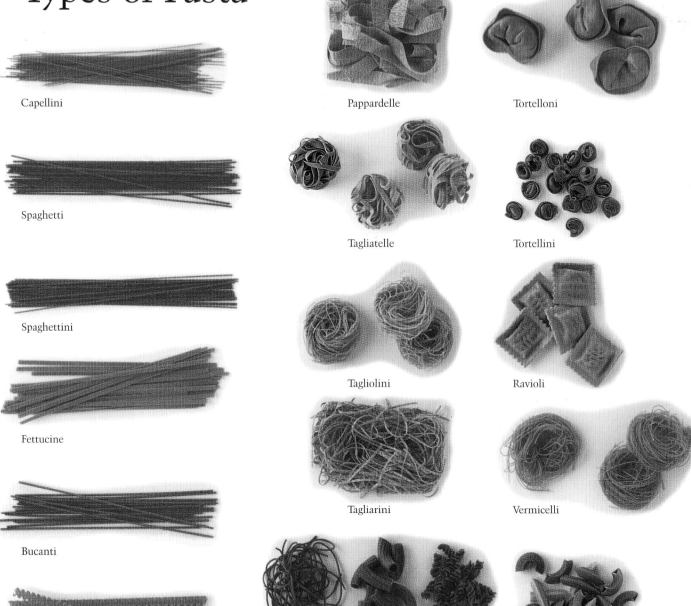

Capellini

Spaghetti

Spaghettini

Fettucine

Bucanti

Lasagnette

Pappardelle

Tagliatelle

Tagliolini

Tagliarini

Flavoured Pasta

Tortelloni

Tortellini

Ravioli

Vermicelli

Coloured Pasta

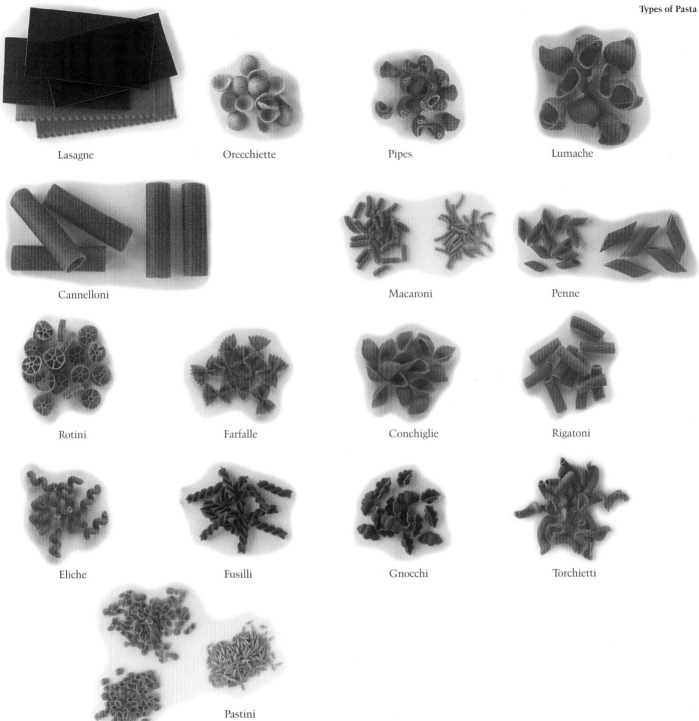

Lasagne

Orecchiette

Pipes

Lumache

Cannelloni

Macaroni

Penne

Rotini

Farfalle

Conchiglie

Rigatoni

Eliche

Fusilli

Gnocchi

Torchietti

Pastini

Soups

Home-made soup is satisfying, comforting and simple to make. You can bulk it up to create a meal in itself or keep it light and enjoy it as a starter or as a stop-gap between meals. There is an Italian proverb which seems quite appropriate: 'a big man can carry a heavy load, and a good soup can carry a dinner'! The Italians make soup using *munnezaglia* – all the leftover pasta in the cupboard. Use your favourite pasta shapes and colours, or buy *pastini* – tiny pasta shapes designed specifically for soups and/or children! Look out for *anelli* (little rings), *stelline* (stars) and *ditalini* (thimbles), and remember that pasta names ending with an '-ini' indicate a smaller version.

Pasta and Basil Soup

Serves 4

Preparation and cooking time:
30 minutes
Calories per serving: 115

Freezing not recommended

V If using vegetable stock

Basil is a sacred herb, native to India but widely used in Italian cooking. In Italy it is a symbol of love – traditionally, a young girl would place a pot of basil in her window as an invitation to her lover to call on her!

2 oz (60 g) vermicelli or spaghetti, broken into short lengths
4 teaspoons olive oil
1 onion, chopped finely
1 garlic clove, chopped finely
½ oz (15 g) pine kernels
1½ pints (900 ml) chicken or vegetable stock
1½ oz (45 g) fresh basil leaves, shredded
salt and freshly ground black pepper
4 teaspoons grated parmesan cheese, to serve

1. Cook the pasta in a large pan of lightly salted boiling water, following the pack instructions. Drain and set aside.
2. Heat the oil in a large saucepan and add the onion, garlic and pine kernels. Cook gently for 10 minutes until the onions are translucent and the pine kernels have turned golden-brown.
3. Add the stock and the basil leaves, bring to a boil and then reduce the heat and simmer for 10 minutes. Add the cooked spaghetti and season to taste with salt and pepper.
4. Spoon the soup into warm bowls and sprinkle a teaspoon of parmesan cheese on top of each serving. Serve at once.

Cook's note:
It is always best to tear or shred basil with your fingers as using a knife can cause the leaves to blacken.

Selections per serving:
½ Carbohydrate; 1 Fat; ½ Vegetable; 25 Optional Calories

Pasta Bean Potage

Serves 4

Preparation time: 15 minutes
Cooking time: 35 minutes
Calories per serving: 195

Freezing recommended

Pasta and Beans (*pasta e fagioli*) is a typical Italian combination. This hearty winter-warmer is a meal in itself. Substitute the cannellini beans with borlotti or haricot beans for a change.

4 teaspoons olive oil
1 onion, chopped finely
1 garlic clove, chopped finely
1 carrot, sliced
1 celery stick, sliced
1 leek, sliced
4 oz (120 g) cooked ham, cut into ½-inch (1 cm) cubes
7 oz (210 g) canned cannellini beans, rinsed and drained
1½ pints (900 ml) chicken stock
2 oz (60 g) pasta spirals
2 large tomatoes, skinned, de-seeded and chopped
1 tablespoon chopped fresh oregano
1 tablespoon chopped fresh marjoram
salt and freshly ground black pepper

1. Heat the oil in a large saucepan. Add the onion, garlic, carrot, celery and leek and cook gently for 5 minutes, stirring occasionally. Add the ham and cook for 5 minutes more.
2. Stir in the beans, stock and pasta spirals. Bring to a boil and then reduce the heat, cover and simmer gently for 20 minutes.
3. Add the tomatoes, oregano and marjoram and simmer gently for 5 minutes more. Season to taste with salt and pepper.
4. Serve, piping hot, in warm soup bowls.

Selections per serving:
1 Carbohydrate; 1 Fat; 1 Protein: 1½ Vegetable; 5 Optional Calories

Minestrone Soup

Serves 4

Preparation time: 15 minutes
Cooking time: 45 minutes
Calories per serving: 155

Freezing recommended

V **If using vegetarian cheese**

Literally meaning 'big soup', minestrone is the king of Italian soups. Traditionally, it would include potatoes and in peasant households, leftover odds and ends would all get thrown into the pot!

4 teaspoons vegetable oil
1 onion, chopped
1 garlic clove, chopped finely
2 carrots, chopped finely
2 celery sticks, sliced
14 oz (420 g) canned chopped tomatoes
2 pints (1.2 litres) vegetable stock
2 oz (60 g) spaghetti, broken into short lengths
4 oz (120 g) frozen peas
6 oz (180 g) green cabbage, shredded
1 leek, sliced finely
1 teaspoon dried basil
4 tablespoons chopped fresh parsley
salt and freshly ground black pepper
4 teaspoons grated parmesan cheese, to serve

1. Heat the oil in a large saucepan. Add the onion and cook gently for 4–5 minutes, until translucent. Add the garlic, carrots and celery and cook for 3 minutes more, stirring occasionally.
2. Add the chopped tomatoes, vegetable stock and spaghetti. Bring to a boil and then cover, reduce the heat and simmer gently for 20 minutes.
3. Add the frozen peas, cabbage, leek, basil and parsley and simmer gently for 20 minutes more. Season to taste with salt and pepper.
4. Ladle the soup into warm bowls and sprinkle a teaspoon of parmesan cheese on top of each. Serve immediately.

Selections per serving:
1/2 Carbohydrate; 1 Fat; 2 1/2 Vegetable; 30 Optional Calories

Variations:
Add 1 oz (30 g) of grilled, chopped lean bacon at step 1. This will add 1/2 Protein Selection per serving and make it unsuitable for vegetarians.

Omit the parmesan cheese and substitute 4 × 1/2 oz (15 g) servings of grated Cheddar cheese. This will add 1/2 Protein Selection and reduce the Optional Calories to 20 per serving.

Mexican Red Pepper and Tomato Soup

Serves 4

Preparation time: 10 minutes
Cooking time: 30 minutes
Calories per serving: 120

Freezing recommended

V

4 teaspoons olive oil
2 onions, sliced
2 red peppers, de-seeded and chopped
2 garlic cloves, crushed
1 tablespoon mild chilli powder
1/2 teaspoon ground cinnamon
14 oz (420 g) canned chopped tomatoes
2 tablespoons tomato purée
1 1/2 pints (900 ml) vegetable stock
4 oz (120 g) cooked macaroni or other small pasta shapes
salt
fresh chopped coriander or oregano, to garnish

1. Heat the oil in a large saucepan. Add the onions, red peppers and garlic and cook gently for about 5 minutes until softened. Stir in the chilli powder and cinnamon and cook for 1 minute more.
2. Add the chopped tomatoes, purée and stock. Bring to a boil and then reduce the heat, cover and simmer for 20 minutes.
3. Blend the soup in a liquidiser or food processor until smooth. Return to the saucepan, add the cooked pasta and reheat the soup gently. Season with salt to taste.
4. Serve the soup in warm bowls, garnished with chopped coriander or oregano.

Selections per serving:
1 Carbohydrate; 1 Fat; 2 Vegetable

Variations:
To make this a more substantial soup, add 6 oz (180 g) canned kidney beans at step 3. This will add 1/2 Protein Selection and increase the Calories to 160 per serving.

Non-vegetarians can add 2 oz (60 g) of finely sliced chorizo sausage at step 3. This also adds 1/2 Protein Selection per serving and increases the Calories to 160 per serving.

Seafood Bisque

Serves 4

Preparation time: 15 minutes
Cooking time: 45 minutes
Calories per serving: 215

Freezing recommended after step 4

Look out for the tiny *conchigliette* pasta – a smaller version of the *conchiglie* (conch shells) or use *maruzze* (seashell) pasta shapes in this delicious soup.

4 teaspoons olive oil
2 onions, sliced
1 lb (480 g) tomatoes, chopped
2 garlic cloves, crushed
1 teaspoon black peppercorns
1 tablespoon chopped fresh oregano
1 tablespoon fresh basil, shredded
1 tablespoon chopped fresh parsley
1¼ pints (750 ml) chicken or fish stock
8 tablespoons tomato purée
2 oz (60 g) small pasta shells
8 oz (240 g) assorted cooked seafood (ie: prawns, crab, mussels and scallops)
2 tablespoons dry sherry
4 teaspoons single cream
salt and freshly ground black pepper
chopped parsley, to garnish

1. Heat the oil in a saucepan. Add the onions and cook gently for 3 minutes. Add the tomatoes, garlic, peppercorns and herbs, and cook gently for 10 minutes or until the tomatoes are soft.
2. Add half the stock, bring to a boil and then reduce the heat, cover and simmer gently for 15 minutes.
3. Strain the soup through a fine sieve, using the back of a wooden spoon to 'press' the vegetables. Discard the vegetables and return the soup to a clean saucepan.
4. Add the remaining stock, tomato purée and pasta. Bring to a boil, and then reduce the heat and simmer for 15 minutes, or until the pasta is *al dente*.
5. Stir in the assorted seafood and the dry sherry and heat through for 5 minutes. Season to taste with salt and pepper.
6. Ladle the soup into warm bowls. Swirl a teaspoon of single cream into each serving. Sprinkle with the chopped parsley and serve at once.

Selections per serving:
½ Carbohydrate; 1 Fat; 1 Protein; 2½ Vegetable; 20 Optional Calories

Chicken and Pasta Broth

Serves 4

Preparation time: 10 minutes
Cooking time: 40 minutes
Calories per serving: 115

Freezing recommended

This clear chicken broth makes a nutritious and light meal in no time at all.

2½ pints (1.5 litres) chicken stock
2 × 3 oz (90 g) boneless, skinless chicken breast
1 teaspoon whole black peppercorns
1 dried bay leaf
1 sprig fresh rosemary or thyme
2 small leeks, sliced
1 carrot, chopped
2 oz (60 g) macaroni
1 small red pepper, de-seeded and chopped
1 tablespoon chopped fresh thyme
salt and freshly ground black pepper
4 teaspoons grated parmesan cheese, to serve

1. Place the stock in a large saucepan and bring to a boil. Add the chicken breasts, peppercorns, bay leaf and sprig of rosemary or thyme. Reduce the heat, cover and simmer gently for 15 minutes.
2. Using a slotted spoon, remove the chicken from the saucepan and leave until cool enough to handle. Strain the stock and return the liquid to the saucepan.
3. Add the leeks, carrot and macaroni to the stock. Bring to a boil and then reduce the heat, cover and simmer gently for 15 minutes.
4. Meanwhile, slice the chicken breasts in small pieces and add them to the broth along with the red pepper. Simmer for 10 minutes more, until the vegetables are tender.
5. Stir in the chopped thyme and season to taste with salt and pepper.
6. Serve in warm soup bowls and sprinkle 1 teaspoon of parmesan cheese over each serving.

Selections per serving:
½ Carbohydrate; 1 Protein; 1 Vegetable; 10 Optional Calories

Light Dishes and Pasta Salads

In this chapter, you will find a selection of pasta dishes which are delicious eaten on their own as a light lunch, as a first course or as an accompaniment to a meal. When you are cooking pasta for cold salads, always drain and rinse it thoroughly under cold running water to prevent it overcooking. Although this washes away the starches that coat the pasta and add flavour to hot pasta dishes, it also prevents it from sticking together. ⤸ Bulk up the recipes with extra vegetables to create a more substantial meal – and don't forget, pasta is ideal for packed lunches and picnics.

Pasta with Ribbons of Courgette and Carrot

Serves 4

Preparation and cooking time: 20 minutes
Calories per serving: 265

Freezing not recommended

V

2 large carrots, peeled
2 large courgettes
8 oz (240 g) pappardelle or lasagnette pasta
4 teaspoons margarine
1/2 teaspoon chopped fresh thyme or marjoram
salt and freshly ground black pepper

1. Top and tail the carrots and courgettes. Using a potato peeler, carefully pare the vegetables into ribbon-like strips.
2. Cook the pasta in plenty of lightly salted boiling water for 8–10 minutes. Two minutes before the end of the cooking time, add the ribbons of carrot and courgette.
3. Drain the cooked pasta and vegetables and toss them with the margarine and chopped herbs. Season with salt and freshly ground black pepper and serve immediately.

Selections per serving:
2 Carbohydrate; 1 Fat; 1 Vegetable

Pasta with Mushrooms

Serves 4

Preparation and cooking time: 20 minutes
Calories per serving: 245

Freezing not recommended

V

Mushrooms are versatile, nutritious and low in Calories, making them the perfect ingredient for many Weight Watchers recipes.

8 oz (240 g) linguine or tagliatelle (egg or spinach flavoured)
4 teaspoons olive oil
2 garlic cloves, chopped
10 oz (300 g) mushrooms, sliced finely
a pinch of grated nutmeg
salt and freshly ground black pepper
1 tablespoon lemon juice
2 tablespoons chopped fresh parsley

1. Cook the pasta in plenty of lightly salted boiling water for 8–10 minutes or until *al dente*.
2. Meanwhile, heat the oil in a large saucepan and gently sauté the garlic for 3–4 minutes. Add the mushrooms and season well with the nutmeg, salt and pepper. Cover and cook over a low heat for 5 minutes. (The mushrooms will release enough moisture to steam in.)
3. Drain the cooked pasta. Stir the lemon juice and parsley into the mushrooms and then carefully fold in the linguine. Serve immediately.

Selections per serving:
2 Carbohydrate; 1 Fat; 1 Vegetable

Variations:
Soak 1/2 oz (15 g) dried mushrooms in 1/2 pint (300 ml) hot water for 30 minutes before adding along with the fresh mushrooms. The flavour is wonderful.

Stir in 4 tablespoons crème fraîche or single cream at step 3. This will add 50 Optional Calories per serving.

Avocado and Orange Pasta Salad

Serves 4

Preparation and cooking time:
30 minutes + 1 hour chilling
Calories per serving: 295

Freezing not recommended

V

6 oz (180 g) pasta bows (*fiochetti*)
   or butterflies (*farfalle*)
2 medium oranges
1 tablespoon olive oil
1 teaspoon white wine vinegar
1 medium avocado
½ oz (15 g) pine kernels, toasted
salt and freshly ground black
   pepper

1. Cook the pasta in plenty of lightly salted boiling water for 8–10 minutes or until *al dente*. Rinse well with cold water and drain thoroughly. Place in a salad bowl.
2. Peel the oranges, carefully removing all the pith. Segment the oranges over a bowl to catch the juices and add the segments to the pasta.
3. Mix the oil and wine vinegar with the reserved orange juice and season with salt and pepper. Carefully spoon the dressing into the pasta, stirring gently to coat. Cover and refrigerate for 1 hour to allow the flavours to develop.
4. Just before serving, peel, quarter and thickly slice the avocado and gently fold it into the pasta. Sprinkle with the toasted pine kernels and serve immediately.

Cook's note:
Sprinkle the sliced avocado with lemon juice to prevent it turning brown.

Selections per serving:
1½ Carbohydrate; 2 Fat; ½ Fruit; 50 Optional Calories

Variations:
Replace the pine kernels with 2 tablespoons of bacon bits. This will reduce the Optional Calories to 45 per serving and make it unsuitable for vegetarians.
   Try substituting the olive oil with hazelnut or walnut oil to add a subtle nutty flavour to the dressing.

Warm Spaghetti Salad with Artichokes

Serves 4

Preparation and cooking time:
20 minutes
Calories per serving: 260

Freezing not recommended

V

Spaghetti derives its name from the Italian word *spago* meaning 'string'. Vermicelli is the *Neapolitan* name describing a thinner spaghetti which is sold in clusters, similar to birds nests.

8 oz (240 g) tricolour spaghetti
4 teaspoons olive oil
1 small onion, halved and
   sliced
6 large black olives, stoned and
   chopped finely
2 teaspoons red wine vinegar
12 oz (360 g) canned artichoke
   hearts, drained and quartered
salt and freshly ground black
   pepper
basil leaves, to garnish

1. Cook the spaghetti in plenty of lightly salted boiling water for 8–10 minutes until *al dente*.
2. Meanwhile, heat the oil in a small saucepan and gently sauté the onion and black olives for 4–5 minutes. Stir in the vinegar and mix together well.
3. Drain the spaghetti and transfer to a salad bowl. Add the artichoke hearts and warm onion and oil dressing. Season with salt and freshly ground black pepper. Toss all the ingredients together and garnish with basil leaves.
4. Serve warm with cold meats or fish or a fresh green salad.

Selections per serving:
2 Carbohydrate; 1 Fat; 1 Vegetable; 10 Optional Calories

Provençal Stuffed Tomatoes

Serves 2

Preparation time: 15 minutes
Cooking time: 20 minutes
Calories per serving: 145

Freezing not recommended

Ripe tomatoes filled with flavours of the Mediterranean – this dish is ideal for lunch or supper and can be prepared well in advance too.

2 oz (60 g) tiny pasta shapes
   (pastini)
4 ripe beef tomatoes
1 small onion, chopped finely
3¹/₂ oz (105 g) canned tuna fish
   in brine, drained
1¹/₂ oz (45 g) canned anchovy
   fillets, drained and chopped
2 tablespoons chopped fresh
   oregano
2 teaspoons capers, chopped
3 large olives, stoned and
   chopped
¹/₂ oz (15 g) parmesan cheese,
   grated
salt and freshly ground black
   pepper

1. Cook the pasta in plenty of lightly salted boiling water for 4–5 minutes until *al dente*. Drain thoroughly and transfer to a bowl. Preheat the oven to Gas Mark 4/180°C/350°F.
2. Slice the top off each tomato and scoop out the pulp and seeds. Reserve the tomato shell, roughly chop the pulp and seeds and toss them with the pasta.
3. Add the onion, tuna fish, anchovies, oregano, capers and olives to the pasta and mix thoroughly. Season to taste with salt and pepper.
4. Carefully spoon the stuffing mixture into the tomato shells and sprinkle with the parmesan cheese.
5. Place the tomatoes in a shallow tray or ovenproof dish and cook for 20–30 minutes or until the tomatoes are tender and the cheese is golden brown. Serve warm.

Cook's note:
For a whimsical garnish, save the tomatoes' lids and use them to 'cap' the baked tomatoes.

Selections per serving:
¹/₂ Carbohydrate; 1¹/₂ Protein; 1 Vegetable; 15 Optional Calories

Variation:
Replace the tuna fish and anchovies with 5 oz (150 g) of cooked chicken breast, chopped finely. This will increase the Protein Selection to 1 and reduce the Optional Calories to 25 per serving.

Greek Pasta Salad

Serves 4

Preparation and cooking time: 25 minutes
Calories per serving: 475

Freezing not recommended

V **If using vegetarian cheese**

This makes a delicious light summer lunch.

6 teaspoons olive oil
1 tablespoon lemon juice
2 teaspoons chopped fresh
   oregano or 1 teaspoon dried
8 oz (240 g) Cheddar cheese,
   cubed
6 large or 10 small black olives,
   stoned and halved
6 oz (180 g) pasta shapes such
   as *farfalle* (butterflies)
4-inch (10 cm) piece of
   cucumber, halved and cut in
   thick slices
1 red or yellow pepper,
   de-seeded and cut in 1-inch
   (2.5 cm) chunks
1 small red onion, sliced
1 gem lettuce, shredded
   (optional)
salt and freshly ground black
   pepper

1. Measure the oil and lemon juice into a large screw-topped jar, add the oregano and season well. Shake the jar to mix the dressing then add the cheese and olives. Give the jar another good shake and leave to marinate for 10–15 minutes.
2. Meanwhile, cook the pasta in a large pan of lightly salted boiling water for 8–10 minutes until just tender. Drain well, rinse with cold water and drain again.
3. Place the cucumber in a large bowl with the pepper, onion, lettuce (if using) and pasta. Add the cheese and olives with the dressing and toss together well. Season to taste with salt and pepper.
4. Divide between 4 plates and serve.

Selections per serving:
1¹/₂ Carbohydrate; 1¹/₂ Fat; 2 Protein; 1¹/₂ Vegetable; 10 Optional Calories

Variation:
Replace the Cheddar cheese with feta cheese, which adds a traditional flavour to this Mediterranean salad. This will reduce the Calories per serving to 400.

Pasta Caponata

Serves 4

Preparation time: 20 minutes
Cooking time: 20 minutes
Calories per serving: 265

Freezing not recommended

**This recipe originates from
southern Italy and is made
from all the ingredients
found in every Italian larder,
or *la dispensa!***

1 aubergine, sliced thickly
1 red pepper
1 yellow pepper
1 tablespoon olive oil
1 onion, cut in chunks
1 garlic clove, chopped
2 tomatoes, skinned and
   chopped
3 tablespoons fresh thyme leaves
2 tablespoons capers, chopped
2 tablespoons red wine vinegar
1 teaspoon brown sugar
8 oz (240 g) pasta twists
   (*eliche*) or spirals (fusilli)
salt and freshly ground black
   pepper

1. Preheat the grill. Lay the aubergine slices on a large chopping board and sprinkle liberally with salt, to extract the bitter juices. Leave for 10 minutes, then turn the slices over and repeat. Place in a colander. Rinse and drain well, then cut the slices in large chunks.
2. Place the peppers under the grill and cook, turning frequently, until the skins have blistered and charred. Carefully transfer the peppers to a bowl. When they are cool enough to handle, remove the skins, de-seed and cut the peppers in squares.
3. Heat the oil in a large, non-stick frying pan. Sauté the aubergine, onion and garlic over a high heat for 3–4 minutes. Add the peppers, tomatoes, thyme, capers, wine vinegar and sugar. Reduce the heat, cover and simmer for 15 minutes.
4. Meanwhile, cook the pasta in plenty of lightly salted boiling water for 8–10 minutes or until *al dente*. Drain and divide between 4 warm bowls.
5. Season the sauce with salt and pepper and spoon over the pasta. Serve immediately.

Cook's note:
Use *eliche* pasta for this pretty dish – twists of pasta which translate as 'propeller'.

Selections per serving:
2 Carbohydrate; ½ Fat; 2 Vegetable; 15 Optional Calories

Variation:
For speed and convenience, use 14 oz (420 g) canned chopped tomatoes and red pimentos (drained) instead of the fresh tomatoes and peppers.

Roast Vegetable Salad

Serves 4

Preparation time: 10–15
minutes
Cooking time: 40–45 minutes
Calories per serving: 245

Freezing not recommended

1 red pepper, de-seeded and cut
   in ½-inch (1 cm) strips
1 green pepper, de-seeded and
   cut in ½-inch (1 cm) strips
1 yellow pepper, de-seeded and
   cut in ½-inch (1 cm) strips

1 aubergine, cut in ½-inch
   (1 cm) thick slices
2 courgettes, cut in ½-inch
   (1 cm) thick slices
2 small unpeeled onions,
   quartered
2–4 large unpeeled garlic cloves
4 teaspoons olive oil
1 tablespoon fresh basil,
   shredded
3–4 tomatoes, quartered
6 oz (180 g) pasta shapes
salt and freshly ground black
   pepper
basil leaves, to garnish

1. Preheat the oven to Gas Mark 6/200°C/400°F.
2. Put the peppers, aubergine, courgettes, onions and garlic in a large roasting tin. Sprinkle with the olive oil and toss in the basil and plenty of salt and freshly ground black pepper. Bake for 20 minutes and then stir the vegetables, add the tomatoes and bake for 20–25 minutes more or until the vegetables are soft and browning.
3. Meanwhile, cook the pasta in a large pan of lightly salted boiling water for 8–10 minutes or until *al dente*. Drain well and squeeze the garlic over the pasta in the colander.
4. Remove the brown outer skins from the onions and discard. Fold the pasta into the vegetables in the roasting tin to soak up all the juices. Check the seasoning and transfer to a warm serving dish. Garnish with basil leaves and serve warm.

Cook's notes:
Fresh sprigs of thyme or oregano could be used instead of basil.
   Baked garlic goes quite soft and loses its pungent taste so don't be afraid to use lots of it!

Selections per serving:
1½ Carbohydrate; 1 Fat; 3 Vegetable

Fragrant Saffron Pasta Salad

Serves 4

Preparation and cooking time:
30 minutes + 1 hour chilling
Calories per serving: 330

Freezing not recommended

V

Use the smallest pasta shapes (*pastini*) you can find for this spicy salad. Italian food shops may stock *orzo* (barley) pasta which resemble grains of rice. This beautifully fragrant and colourful salad is a good accompaniment to barbecued chicken or lamb.

8 oz (240 g) small pasta shapes
4 teaspoons olive oil
a pinch of pure saffron powder
    or strands
1 oz (30 g) flaked almonds
2 oz (60 g) currants
1 garlic clove, crushed
juice of 1 lime
1 teaspoon clear honey
1/4 teaspoon ground cumin
1/4 teaspoon ground coriander
1/2 yellow pepper, de-seeded and
    cut into slivers
1 tablespoon finely chopped
    fresh parsley
1 tablespoon finely chopped
    fresh mint
1 tablespoon finely chopped
    fresh coriander
salt and freshly ground black
    pepper
fresh coriander leaves, to garnish

1. Cook the pasta in plenty of lightly salted boiling water for a few minutes less than the pack instructions. Rinse well with cold water and drain thoroughly. Transfer to a serving bowl.
2. Heat the oil in a small saucepan and add the saffron, flaked almonds, currants and garlic. Cook gently, stirring, until the almonds turn a rich nutty brown. Remove from the heat and blend in the lime juice, honey, cumin and coriander.
3. Gently fold the pasta, pepper slivers and fresh herbs into the dressing until lightly coated. Season to taste with salt and pepper.
4. Refrigerate for 1 hour and then serve the salad, garnished with sprigs of fresh coriander.

Selections per serving:
2 Carbohydrate; 1 1/2 Fat; 1/2 Fruit; 1/4 Vegetable; 20 Optional Calories

Pasta Salad with Rocket and Tomato Dressing

Serves 4

Preparation and cooking time:
20 minutes + 2 hours chilling
Calories per serving: 240

Freezing not recommended

V

You don't have to travel to Italy to enjoy wild *rughetta*, a spiky green-leaved plant with a strong peppery flavour. Most supermarkets now sell rocket, a slightly milder cultivated variety. If you can't find it, use spinach or a mixture of lamb's lettuce and watercress.

4 ripe tomatoes, peeled,
    de-seeded and chopped finely
2 garlic cloves, chopped finely
2 oz (60 g) rocket leaves,
    chopped coarsely
1 tablespoon olive oil
8 oz (240 g) penne (quills)
salt and freshly ground black
    pepper

1. Place the tomatoes, garlic and rocket leaves in a bowl. Add the olive oil and season well with the salt and pepper. Cover and refrigerate for at least 2 hours.
2. Cook the pasta in plenty of lightly salted boiling water for 8–10 minutes until *al dente*. Rinse well with cold water and drain thoroughly. Toss the pasta with the chilled tomato mixture and serve.

Cook's notes:
Serve this salad warm – simply toss the hot, drained pasta into the chilled tomato sauce.
   If they are available, plum tomatoes taste delicious in this recipe.

Selections per serving:
2 Carbohydrate; 1/2 Fat; 1 Vegetable; 10 Optional Calories

Variation:
Sprinkle each serving with 1/2 oz (15 g) grated parmesan cheese. This will add 1/2 Protein Selection per serving and increase the Calories to 270 per serving.

Pasta Sauces

Nothing could be more simple or delicious than a bowl of your favourite pasta topped with a tasty, colourful sauce. However, pasta has had to shake off its reputation as a fattening food – quite unfair when all along, it was the sauce you tossed it into! This chapter offers a good variety of sauces which fit into the Programme and can be varied simply by adding different herbs or vegetables. Remember, long thin pasta such as tagliatelle or spaghetti is ideal with creamy cheese sauces, while shapes and tubes (*farfalle*, *fusilli*) go well with heavier vegetable sauces. Choose your favourites and don't forget to add the Carbohydrate Selections to your daily menu planner!

Basic White Sauce

Makes 3/4 pint (450 ml) or 4 servings

Preparation and cooking time: 10 minutes
Calories per serving: 90

Freezing not recommended

V

This sauce makes an ideal base in which to add your favourite ingredients and flavours – so long as they fit into the Programme! For example, cooked chicken, tuna, salmon and dill, cheese, salami and black olives, chopped tomatoes – the combinations are endless.

1 tablespoon margarine
1 oz (30 g) plain flour
3/4 pint (450 ml) skimmed milk
salt and freshly ground black pepper

1. Place the margarine, flour and milk in a saucepan. Heat gently, stirring constantly with a wire whisk until the sauce starts to boil and thicken.
2. Reduce the heat and cook for 2–3 minutes. Season with salt and pepper to taste, or flavour with any additional ingredients you have chosen.

Selections per serving:
1/2 Fat; 1/4 Milk; 40 Optional Calories

Creamy Cheese Dressing

Serves 2

Preparation time: 5 minutes
Calories per serving: 155

Freezing not recommended

V

This quick dressing is delicious tossed into hot or cold pasta, and will keep for several days in the refrigerator.

4 oz (120 g) cottage cheese
4 teaspoons sunflower oil
4 teaspoons lemon juice
2 tablespoons dry white wine
2 teaspoons Dijon mustard
1 teaspoon chopped fresh dill or tarragon
1 teaspoon snipped chives
salt and freshly ground black pepper

1. Place all the ingredients in a food processor and blend until smooth.
2. Season to taste with salt and pepper and chill until required.

Cook's note:
Toss your favourite vegetables along with some pasta into this creamy dressing to make a delicious and healthy meal.

Selections per serving:
2 Fat; 1 Protein; 15 Optional Calories

Neapolitan Tomato Sauce

Serves 4

Preparation time: 10 minutes
Cooking time: 40 minutes
Calories per serving: 45

Freezing recommended

$\mathcal{V}$

Here is a good basic full-flavoured sauce. The Neapolitans are famous for their tomatoes, which have been an essential fresh ingredient in their cookery since the 16th century. Canned tomatoes were first produced and exported from Italy in the early 1900's and have become a popular timesaver for cooks everywhere.

2 teaspoons vegetable oil
1 onion, chopped finely
1 stick celery, chopped (optional)
24 oz (720 g) canned chopped tomatoes
1 teaspoon dried basil
1 teaspoon sugar
2 tablespoons chopped fresh parsley
salt and freshly ground black pepper

1. Heat the oil in a saucepan and cook the onion and celery (if using) gently for 3–4 minutes, or until softened.
2. Add the chopped tomatoes, basil, sugar and salt and pepper. Bring to a boil, then reduce the heat and simmer uncovered for 20–30 minutes, or until the sauce has reduced and thickened. Adjust the seasoning to taste.
3. Stir in the parsley and serve with hot pasta.

Selections per serving:
$\frac{1}{2}$ Fat; $2\frac{1}{2}$ Vegetable; 5 Optional Calories

Variation:
Simply add your favourite herbs, some chopped mushrooms or tuna fish to the sauce to create endless combinations, not forgetting to add the extra Selections of course!

Uncooked Tomato Sauce

Serves 2

Preparation time: 10 minutes + 24 hours chilling
Calories per serving: 145

Freezing not recommended

$\mathcal{V}$

Plan ahead with this sauce; make it one or two days beforehand to allow the flavours to develop. Plum tomatoes are particularly flavourful if you can find them.

6 tomatoes, chopped finely
1 onion, chopped finely
2 garlic cloves, chopped finely
3 tablespoons fresh basil, shredded
1 tablespoon chopped fresh oregano or 1 teaspoon dried oregano
1 tablespoon chopped fresh parsley or 1 teaspoon dried parsley
1–2 teaspoons sugar
1 tablespoon lemon juice
4 teaspoons olive oil
salt and freshly ground black pepper

1. Place the tomatoes, onion, garlic and herbs in a bowl. Stir in 1 teaspoon of sugar, the lemon juice, olive oil and salt and pepper.
2. Cover and refrigerate for at least 24 hours. Adjust the seasoning to taste, adding salt and pepper and the remaining sugar if necessary.
3. Gently heat the sauce and serve with hot pasta, or mix with cold cooked pasta and serve as a salad.

Cook's note:
Remember, 1 oz (30 g) uncooked pasta or 3 oz (90 g) cooked pasta equals 1 Carbohydrate Selection.

Selections per serving:
2 Fat; 3 Vegetable; 20–40 Optional Calories (depending on the amount of sugar used)

Garlic and Mushroom Sauce

Serves 2

Preparation and cooking time:
20 minutes
Calories per serving: 115

Freezing not recommended

V

Smoked garlic adds a subtle, exotic flavour to this mushroom sauce. Many supermarkets now stock it – but if it is difficult to find, ordinary garlic is just as delicious.

2 teaspoons olive oil
1 onion, sliced finely
3 garlic cloves, chopped finely (smoked if available)
8 oz (240 g) mushrooms, wiped and chopped
1/2 teaspoon paprika
2 oz (60 g) low-fat soft cheese
salt and freshly ground black pepper

1. Heat the oil in a large saucepan and sauté the onion and garlic over a medium heat until golden. Add the mushrooms and cook gently for 10 minutes, stirring occasionally, until the mushrooms are soft.
2. Remove the saucepan from the heat and stir in the paprika and soft cheese. Season well with salt and pepper.
3. Toss the sauce in with your favourite pasta and serve hot.

Cook's note:
Experiment with different varieties of mushrooms – shiitake, oyster and chanterelle. They each have their own unique texture and flavour.

Selections per serving:
1 Fat; 1/2 Protein; 2 Vegetable

Sweet Red Pepper Sauce

Serves 4

Preparation time: 10 minutes
Cooking time: 25 minutes
Calories per serving: 45

Freezing recommended

V **If using vegetable stock**

2 red peppers
2 teaspoons olive oil
1 onion, chopped finely
8 oz (240 g) tomatoes, skinned and chopped
1 garlic clove, crushed
1/2 teaspoon dried thyme
1/2 teaspoon ground cinnamon
1/2 pint (300 ml) vegetable or chicken stock
1 tablespoon tomato purée
salt and freshly ground black pepper
chopped parsley or basil, to garnish

1. Preheat the grill to its highest setting. Place the whole peppers under the grill and turn them regularly until the skins have charred all over. This will make them easier to peel. Carefully set them aside to cool.
2. Heat the oil in a saucepan and cook the onion gently until softened but not coloured. Add the tomatoes, garlic, thyme and cinnamon and cook for a further 10 minutes.
3. Meanwhile, peel the skins off the peppers and discard them along with the stalks and seeds. Roughly chop the peppers and add them to the pan along with the stock and tomato purée. Bring the sauce to a boil and simmer for 10 minutes.
4. Purée or sieve the sauce until smooth. Return to the rinsed pan and heat through. Season with salt and pepper and serve hot with pasta, garnished with the chopped parsley or basil.

Selections per serving:
1/2 Fat; 2 Vegetable

Variation:
Slice 6 large pitted black olives and add them to the sauce during step 4. This will add 10 Optional Calories per serving and increase the Calories per serving to 50.

Spinach and Ricotta Cheese Sauce

Serves 4

Preparation and cooking time:
15 minutes
Calories per serving: 130

Freezing not recommended

$\mathcal{V}$

Ricotta cheese is very popular in Italian cooking and is used in both savoury and dessert recipes. It is a smooth and milky unripened cheese similar in taste and texture to cottage cheese.

3 teaspoons margarine
½ small onion, chopped finely
1 lb (480 g) fresh spinach, chopped
½ teaspoon chopped fresh thyme
4 oz (120 g) ricotta cheese
a pinch of freshly grated nutmeg
½ oz (15 g) pine kernels, toasted
salt and freshly ground black pepper

1. Melt the margarine in a saucepan and sauté the onion over a gentle heat until soft but not browned.
2. Add the spinach and thyme and continue to cook gently for 2–3 minutes or until the spinach leaves have wilted.
3. Beat in the ricotta cheese with a wooden spoon, to form a smooth sauce. Season to taste, with the nutmeg, salt and pepper.
4. Divide the sauce between 4 bowls of cooked pasta. Sprinkle the pine kernels equally on to each portion. Serve at once.

Selections per serving:
1 Fat; 1 Protein; 1½ Vegetable; 10 Optional Calories

Variation:
Substitute the pine kernels with 4 teaspoons of bacon bits. This will reduce the Fat Selection to ½ and make the dish unsuitable for vegetarians. It will also add an additional 10 Optional Calories per serving and the Calories per serving will decrease to 115.

Amatriciana Sauce

Serves 4

Preparation time: 10 minutes
Cooking time: 25 minutes
Calories per serving: 145

Freezing recommended

A fiery sauce originating from Amatrice, a town in central Italy famous for rearing and butchering pigs. Toss it into cooked spaghetti or penne, and have a crisp green salad on stand-by to cool down the palate!

4 oz (120 g) lean back bacon rashers
2 teaspoons vegetable oil
1 large onion, sliced finely
14 oz (420 g) canned chopped tomatoes
½–1 red chilli, de-seeded and chopped finely
salt and freshly ground black pepper
1 tablespoon chopped fresh parsley (optional)

1. Trim any fat from the bacon. Cut the rashers in strips.
2. Heat the oil in a saucepan and gently sauté the onion until soft and translucent. Add the bacon, tomatoes and chilli, and simmer uncovered for 25 minutes, stirring occasionally. Season to taste with salt and pepper and stir in the parsley, if using.
3. Mix the sauce into cooked pasta and serve immediately.

Cook's note:
Take care when handling fresh chillies. Do not touch your eyes or mouth before washing your hands thoroughly.

Selections per serving:
½ Fat; 2 Protein; 1½ Vegetable

Yogurt and Herb Sauce

Serves 2

Preparation time: 10 minutes
Cooking time: 10 minutes
Calories per serving: 250

Freezing not recommended

V

This very light, aromatic sauce
is delicious when mixed in
with tricolour (*mista tricolore*)
pasta spirals or bows.

2 teaspoons margarine
1 shallot, chopped finely
1 garlic clove, crushed

¹/₂ oz (15 g) plain flour
6 tablespoons vegetable stock
5 fl oz (150 ml) low-fat natural
    yogurt
2 tablespoons cream cheese
2 tablespoons chopped fresh
    parsley
2 tablespoons snipped fresh
    chives
2 tablespoons fresh basil,
    shredded
salt and freshly ground black
    pepper
¹/₂ oz (15 g) pine kernels, lightly
    toasted, to serve

1. Melt the margarine in a medium-sized saucepan and gently sauté
the shallot and garlic until softened but not browned. Sprinkle in the
flour and continue to cook, stirring, for 1–2 minutes.
2. Gradually blend in the stock and bring to a boil, stirring
constantly, until the sauce thickens.
3. Remove from the heat, stir in the low-fat yogurt and cream cheese,
and gently warm through over a low heat for 2 minutes. Do not allow
the sauce to boil.
4. Stir in the herbs and season the sauce with salt and pepper.
Spoon the sauce over individual bowls of hot pasta and sprinkle
with the toasted pine kernels.

Cook's note:
Remember that 3 oz (90 g) of cooked pasta equals 1 Carbohydrate
Selection.

Selections per serving:
1¹/₂ Fat; ¹/₂ Milk; 85 Optional Calories

Italian Pasta Dressing

Serves 4

Preparation time: 10 minutes
+ 2 days marinating
Calories per serving: 100

Freezing not recommended

V

This is a delicious dressing
which needs to be made
ahead, but will keep in the
refrigerator for up to 7 days –
so it is ideal for a quick mid-
week supper when the pressure
is on! Serve it tossed into hot
or cold pasta, and add some
cooked fish or chicken if
you're very hungry. (Remember
to add the appropriate Protein
Selections.)

1 oz (30 g) fresh basil leaves
    (without coarse stalks)
1 tablespoon fresh white
    breadcrumbs, toasted
1 garlic clove
¹/₂ teaspoon coriander seeds
1 tablespoon chopped dill
1 teaspoon chopped rosemary
2 large tomatoes, skinned and
    de-seeded
¹/₂ teaspoon paprika
3 tablespoons tomato juice
3 tablespoons olive oil
salt and freshly ground black
    pepper

1. Place the basil leaves, breadcrumbs, garlic and coriander seeds in
a food processor and blend until smooth.
2. Add the dill, rosemary, tomatoes and paprika and work the
ingredients to a fine paste.
3. Add the tomato juice and oil and continue to blend until
smooth. Season well with salt and pepper.
4. Transfer to a screw-top jar or bowl, cover and refrigerate for
several days before using.

Cook's note:
Extra virgin olive oil is very green and has a stronger flavour than
the more refined virgin oil. It is the oil from the first pressing of the
olives and is used mainly for dressing salads and cold antipasta. Try
it in this recipe for an extra special dressing.

Selections per serving:
2 Fat; ¹/₂ Vegetable; 20 Optional Calories

Variation:
Omit the paprika and add half a red chilli for a really spicy
dressing.

Pasta with Eggs and Cheese

Pasta and cheese are a great combination which allow you to linger over the flavour of the cheese. Why not choose your favourite cheese and alter the recipe to suit? Try tomato and garlic flavoured pastas with cheese and egg-based sauces. The flavours combine deliciously, and the colours look great against the creamy sauces. ⌇⌇ The bakes and gratins are satisfying meals that the whole family will enjoy.

Pasta with Blue Cheese Dressing

Serves 2

Preparation and cooking time: 15 minutes
Calories per serving: 425

Freezing not recommended

V **If using vegetarian cheese**

4 oz (120 g) ribbon-type pasta (ie: pappardelle, fettucine or tagliatelle)

8 oz (240 g) leeks, trimmed and sliced finely
2 oz (60 g) dolcelatte or Stilton cheese, crumbled
2 oz (60 g) 8% fat fromage frais
2 teaspoons snipped fresh chives or finely chopped spring onions
1/2 oz (15 g) chopped walnuts, toasted
salt and freshly ground black pepper

1. Cook the pasta in a saucepan of lightly salted boiling water for about 5 minutes or according to pack instructions, then add the leeks and cook for 2 minutes more. Drain well.
2. In a large bowl, mix the dolcelatte or Stilton cheese with the fromage frais and chives. Season with salt and freshly ground black pepper.
3. Fold the pasta and leeks into the cheese and herb mixture. Divide into 2 bowls and sprinkle the walnuts evenly over each serving.

Selections per serving:
2 Carbohydrate; 1/2 Fat; 1 1/2 Protein; 1 1/2 Vegetable; 15 Optional Calories

Variation:
Sprinkle with 2 teaspoons of bacon bits at step 3. This will add 10 Optional Calories per serving and make it unsuitable for vegetarians.

Spaghetti Carbonara

Serves 2

Preparation and cooking time: 25 minutes
Calories per serving: 425

Freezing not recommended

This famous dish is said to be named after the local coalmen or charcoal makers – the *carbonari*. Because little cooking and few ingredients are needed for this dish, it was easily cooked over an open fire.

2 oz (60 g) smoked lean back bacon rashers
1 teaspoon olive oil
1 small onion or shallot, chopped finely
1 garlic clove, crushed
1 tablespoon wine vinegar
4 oz (120 g) spaghetti
2 eggs, size 1
4 teaspoons grated parmesan cheese
2 tablespoons single cream
salt and freshly ground black pepper

1. Trim the bacon of any fat and cut in strips.
2. Heat the oil in a small pan and quickly cook the onion or shallot, garlic and bacon for 5 minutes until the onion or shallot is softened. Add the vinegar, and cook for 2 minutes more. Set aside.
3. Meanwhile, cook the spaghetti in a large saucepan of lightly salted boiling water for 8–10 minutes.
4. In a small bowl whisk the eggs and beat in the parmesan and cream. Season to taste with salt and plenty of ground black pepper. Drain the spaghetti in a colander, put it back into the pan and pour in the beaten eggs. Add the bacon and onion sauce and mix well. If the eggs do not scramble by the heat of the pasta, place the pan over a low heat and cook for a few minutes, stirring constantly, until very lightly cooked.
5. Divide the spaghetti between 2 warm bowls and serve.

Selections per serving:
2 Carbohydrate; 1/2 Fat; 3 Protein; 70 Optional Calories

(V) **Vegetarian option:**
Omit the bacon and substitute 2 oz (60 g) of button mushrooms. This will reduce the Protein Selection to 1 and the Calories per serving to 375.

Lasagnette with Cheese and Onion Sauce

Serves 2

Preparation time: 10 minutes
Cooking time: 45 minutes
Calories per serving: 580

Freezing not recommended

$\mathcal{V}$ **If using vegetarian cheese**

There is an Italian saying –
come il cacia sui maccheroni –
'like cheese on pasta'. In
other words, the two are
inseparable. Taste this and
you are sure to agree!

4 teaspoons vegetable oil
8 oz (240 g) onions, sliced
  thickly
4 oz (120 g) lasagnette or
  pappardelle pasta
1 tablespoon chopped parsley
1 egg, beaten
3 oz (90 g) Emmental cheese,
  grated
1 oz (30 g) Sbrinz cheese,
  grated
salt and freshly ground black
  pepper

1. Heat the oil in a covered saucepan and cook the onions gently over a low heat for 35–40 minutes. They will become very soft and sweet.
2. Ten minutes before the onions are ready, cook the pasta in plenty of lightly salted boiling water for 8–10 minutes or until *al dente*. Drain and transfer to a warm bowl.
3. Season the onions with salt and pepper. Increase the heat and cook, stirring occasionally, for 5 minutes more or until the onions turn a rich golden colour. Remove from the heat, stir in the parsley and quickly whisk in the egg. Cover and let stand for 1 or 2 minutes.
4. Toss the onion mixture and the grated Emmental into the pasta. Divide between 2 warm bowls and sprinkle with the Sbrinz cheese. Serve immediately.

Cook's notes:
Try and use Spanish onions for this recipe as they are much sweeter and milder than our standard white onions.
   Edam and parmesan cheese can be used instead of Emmental and Sbrinz with equally tasty results!

Selections per serving:
2 Carbohydrate; 2 Fat; 2 Protein; 1½ Vegetable; 30 Optional Calories

Nutty Cheese and Gnocchi Bake

Serves 4

Preparation time: 20 minutes
Cooking time: 20 minutes
Calories per serving: 440

Freezing recommended

$\mathcal{V}$ **If using vegetarian cheese**

Gnocchi can refer to two
different Italian foods. In this
recipe, it is the name given to
the pasta shape. This, in turn,
probably derives its name
from the little dumplings
called gnocchi, made from
flour or polenta, spinach and
ricotta cheese.

8 oz (240 g) gnocchi or pasta
  shells
4 teaspoons margarine
1 onion, chopped
1 oz (30 g) plain flour
½ pint (300 ml) skimmed milk
2 tablespoons tomato purée
1 oz (30 g) toasted hazelnuts,
  chopped
8 oz (240 g) cottage cheese
1 oz (30 g) Cheshire or
  Lancashire cheese, grated
salt and freshly ground black
  pepper
To garnish:
parsley
tomato slices

1. Cook the pasta in plenty of lightly salted boiling water for 8–10 minutes until it is just *al dente*. Drain thoroughly. Preheat the oven to Gas Mark 5/190°C/375°F.
2. Meanwhile, melt the margarine in a medium-sized saucepan and cook the onion over a gentle heat for 5 minutes until softened but not coloured. Sprinkle in the flour and cook, stirring constantly, for 1 minute more.
3. Add the milk gradually and bring to a boil, stirring constantly with a wire whisk, until the sauce thickens. Remove the saucepan from the heat and stir in the tomato purée, hazelnuts, cottage cheese and lastly, the cooked pasta. Season to taste with salt and pepper.
4. Pour the mixture into a 2-pint (1.2 litre) ovenproof dish and sprinkle the grated cheese evenly over the surface. Bake for 20 minutes, until the top is golden. Garnish with the parsley and tomato slices and serve immediately.

Selections per serving:
2 Carbohydrate; 2 Fat; ¼ Milk; 1 Protein; ½ Vegetable;
35 Optional Calories

Ratatouille Pasta Gratin

Serves 4

Preparation time: 30 minutes
Cooking time: 40 minutes
Calories per serving: 350

Freezing recommended

𝒱 **If using vegetarian cheese**

1 small aubergine, cubed
8 oz (240 g) wholewheat pasta
   shapes (ie: shells or
   macaroni)
1 onion, chopped
1 garlic clove, crushed
1 green pepper, de-seeded and
   sliced

1 yellow pepper, de-seeded and
   sliced
3 courgettes, sliced
14 oz (420 g) canned chopped
   tomatoes
2 tablespoons tomato purée
2 teaspoons fresh chopped
   oregano
2 teaspoons fresh basil,
   shredded
4 oz (120 g) mozzarella cheese,
   grated
salt and freshly ground black
   pepper

1. Spread the aubergine out on a plate and sprinkle liberally with salt to extract the bitter juices. Leave for 20 minutes. Place in a colander and rinse and drain well.
2. Meanwhile, cook the pasta in plenty of lightly salted boiling water for 12–15 minutes until just tender. Drain thoroughly.
3. Place the aubergines, onion, garlic, peppers, courgettes, canned tomatoes and purée together in a large saucepan. Gently bring to a boil, then reduce the heat, cover and simmer for 20 minutes. Shake the pan and stir the vegetables occasionally to prevent them from sticking.
4. Preheat the oven to Gas Mark 5/190°C/375°F.
5. Season the vegetables with salt and pepper and stir in the fresh herbs and the cooked pasta. Spoon into a ovenproof gratin dish. Sprinkle the grated cheese over the surface and bake for 20 minutes until golden and bubbling. Serve immediately.

Cook's note:
This dish, served hot or cold (as suggested below) makes a delicious accompaniment to either chicken or poached salmon.

Selections per serving:
2 Carbohydrate; 1 Protein; 2½ Vegetable;

Variation:
Omit the cheese and refrigerate after adding the herbs and pasta to enjoy this dish as a cold salad. This will remove the Protein Selection and reduce the Calories to 260 per serving.

Spaghetti Fritatta

Serves 4

Preparation time: 20 minutes
Cooking time: 15 minutes
Calories per serving: 390

Freezing not recommended

𝒱 **If using vegetarian cheese**

Fritatta – an Italian omelette – is the ideal way to use up leftover cooked pasta. As with a regular omelette, you can add chopped mushrooms, ham, vegetables, or even leftover sauces to the pasta and egg mixture. Serve it warm with a crisp green salad. Replace the fresh herbs with 1 teaspoon of mixed dried herbs.

4 teaspoons vegetable oil
1 onion, chopped finely
4 eggs, beaten
2 tomatoes, skinned, de-seeded
   and chopped
4 button mushrooms, wiped
   and chopped (optional)
2 tablespoons double cream
8 oz (240 g) cooked spaghetti
   or taglierini
1 teaspoon chopped parsley
1 teaspoon snipped chives
1 teaspoon chopped marjoram
2 oz (60 g) parmesan cheese,
   grated
2 oz (60 g) Gruyère or mature
   Cheddar cheese, grated
salt and freshly ground black
   pepper
a sprig of fresh basil, to garnish

1. Heat the oil in a non-stick frying pan and sauté the onion over a medium heat for 5 minutes until golden. Preheat the grill.
2. Mix together the eggs, tomatoes, mushrooms (if using), cream, cooked pasta, herbs and parmesan cheese. Season well with salt and pepper. Pour the egg mixture into the hot frying pan with the onions, lower the heat and cook gently for 6–8 minutes or until the eggs have just set.
3. Sprinkle the grated Gruyère cheese evenly over the surface of the fritatta and grill for 2–3 minutes or until the cheese is melted and bubbling.
4. Slide the frittata on to a serving plate or board and garnish with a sprig of fresh basil. Cut into quarters and serve warm.

Selections per serving:
½ Carbohydrate; 1 Fat; 2 Protein; ½ Vegetable; 35 Optional Calories

Cheese and Tomato Pasta Flan

Serves 4

Preparation time: 40 minutes
Cooking time: 30 minutes
Calories per serving: 355

Freezing not recommended

V **If using vegetarian cheese**

6 oz (180 g) taglierini or
   spaghettini
2 eggs
a pinch of grated nutmeg
1 oz (30 g) parmesan cheese,
   grated
4 teaspoons olive oil
1 small onion, chopped
1 garlic clove, crushed
28 oz (840 g) canned chopped
   tomatoes, drained
1 teaspoon sugar
1 tablespoon fresh chopped
   oregano
1 tablespoon fresh basil,
   shredded
3 oz (90 g) mozzarella cheese,
   sliced thinly
salt and freshly ground black
   pepper
fresh basil, to garnish

1. Preheat the oven to Gas Mark 5/190°C/375°F. Cook the pasta in plenty of lightly salted boiling water for 8–10 minutes or until *al dente*. Drain thoroughly.
2. Beat together the eggs, nutmeg and parmesan cheese. Season well with salt and pepper. Add the cooked pasta and stir well to coat.
3. Grease an 8-inch (20 cm) round pie dish with a little of the olive oil. Press the pasta and egg mixture evenly over the base and up the sides of the dish to form a shallow rim. Cook in the oven for 10 minutes or until the pasta case has lightly set.
4. Meanwhile, heat the remaining oil in a saucepan and gently cook the onion and garlic for 4–5 minutes. Add the drained tomatoes and simmer for 15 minutes or until the sauce has reduced and thickened to a pulpy consistency.
5. Season thoroughly with the sugar and salt and pepper. Stir in the oregano and basil.
6. Layer half of the mozzarella slices on to the base of the pasta case, pour on the tomato sauce and arrange the remaining cheese slices over the top.
7. Bake in the oven for 25–30 minutes or until the cheese has turned golden. Garnish with the fresh basil.

Cook's note:
If the outside edge of the flan begins to brown before the centre is ready, cover the rim with a strip of kitchen foil.

Selections per serving:
1½ Carbohydrate; 1 Fat; 1½ Protein; 2½ Vegetable; 5 Optional Calories

Mushroom and Spinach Gratin

Serves 4

Preparation time: 25 minutes
Cooking time: 20 minutes
Calories per serving: 385

Freezing recommended

V **If using vegetarian cheese**

4 oz (120 g) (6 sheets) egg
   lasagne
4 teaspoons vegetable oil
1 small onion, chopped finely
1 garlic clove, chopped finely
1 lb (480 g) button mushrooms,
   wiped and chopped finely
12 oz (360 g) frozen spinach,
   thawed and squeezed dry
a pinch of grated nutmeg
¼ pint (150 ml) water
1 oz (30 g) low-fat dried milk
   powder
4 teaspoons cornflour
½ pint (300 ml) skimmed milk
4 oz (120 g) Gruyère or mature
   Cheddar cheese, grated
salt and freshly ground black
   pepper

1. Cook the lasagne sheets in plenty of lightly salted boiling water for 8–10 minutes or until *al dente*. Remove carefully with a slotted spoon and spread in a single layer on a large chopping board.
2. Heat the vegetable oil in a large saucepan and gently cook the onion, garlic and mushrooms for 5–6 minutes. Stir in the spinach and cook briskly for 2 minutes to allow any excess liquid to evaporate. Season well with the nutmeg and salt and pepper.
3. Spread the mixture evenly over the sheets of lasagne and roll each sheet up from a long side. Using a very sharp knife, carefully cut each roll into three even pieces. Pack the rolls tightly together, standing upright in a deep ovenproof dish.
4. Preheat the oven to Gas Mark 6/200°C/400°F. Make a paste with the water, dried milk powder and cornflour. Heat the skimmed milk in a small saucepan and bring to a boil, whisk in the cornflour paste and stir constantly until the sauce thickens. Reduce the heat and simmer for 1 minute.
5. Fold in about half of the grated cheese, stirring until it has melted. Season the sauce with salt and pepper and pour over the pasta rolls. Sprinkle with the remaining cheese and bake for 20 minutes until golden and bubbly.

Selections per serving:
1 Carbohydrate; 1 Fat; ½ Milk; 1 Protein; 3 Vegetable; 10 Optional Calories

Leek, Bean and Caerphilly Bake

Serves 4

Preparation time: 20 minutes
Cooking time: 30 minutes
Calories per serving: 385

Freezing recommended

$\mathcal{V}$ **If using vegetarian cheese**

4 oz (120 g) frozen broad beans
4 oz (120 g) tricolour pasta
shapes (ie: gnocchi or shell)

4 teaspoons margarine
12 oz (360 g) leeks, trimmed
and sliced
1 oz (30 g) plain flour
1 pint (600 ml) skimmed milk
4 oz (120 g) Caerphilly cheese,
crumbled
2 tablespoons chopped parsley
1/2 oz (15 g) fresh breadcrumbs
salt and freshly ground black
pepper

1. Bring a large saucepan of lightly salted water to a boil. Add the frozen broad beans and bring back to the boil. Add the pasta and cook for 8–10 minutes until the pasta and beans are just tender. Drain well.
2. Melt the margarine in a pan and sauté the leeks gently for 3–4 minutes. Sprinkle in the flour and cook, stirring, for 1 minute more. Reduce the heat and blend in the milk gradually. Bring to a boil and cook, stirring, for 2 minutes.
3. Preheat the oven to Gas Mark 5/190°C/375°F.
4. Remove the saucepan from the heat and stir in half the cheese along with the parsley, pasta and broad beans. Season with salt and pepper.
5. Spoon the mixture into a 2 pint (1.2 litre) ovenproof dish. Sprinkle the remaining cheese and the breadcrumbs evenly over the surface. Bake for 30 minutes or until golden and bubbling. Serve immediately.

Selections per serving:
1 1/2 Carbohydrate; 1 Fat; 1/2 Milk; 1 Protein; 1 Vegetable;
10 Optional Calories

Variation:
Try a blue cheese – Stilton or Blue Shropshire – for a very different, but equally delicious sauce.

Macaroni and Cauliflower Cheese

Serves 4

Preparation time: 20 minutes
Cooking time: 25 minutes
Calories per serving: 345

Freezing not recommended

$\mathcal{V}$ **If using vegetarian cheese**

You can still see women in Italy sitting on doorsteps making *maccheroni* by the traditional method. Tiny pieces of pasta are wrapped around knitting needles or willow branches to form the miniature tubes which we know as macaroni.

1 small cauliflower, broken into
florets
4 oz (120 g) macaroni
2 teaspoons margarine
1 small onion, chopped finely
1 oz (30 g) plain flour
1 pint (600 ml) skimmed milk
4 oz (120 g) mature Cheddar
cheese
a pinch of dry mustard
salt and freshly ground black
pepper

1. Preheat the oven to Gas Mark 5/190°C/375°F.
2. Cook the cauliflower and pasta separately in lightly salted boiling water for 8–10 minutes, or until just tender. Drain both thoroughly, transfer to a 2 pint (1.2 litre) ovenproof gratin dish and stir gently to mix.
3. Meanwhile, melt the margarine in a medium-size saucepan. Add the onion and cook gently for 4–5 minutes until softened, but not browned. Remove from the heat and stir in the flour. Cook gently for 1 minute more and blend in the milk gradually. Return to the heat, stirring constantly until the sauce boils and thickens. Remove from the heat.
4. Stir 3 oz (90 g) of the cheese into the sauce. Add the mustard and salt and pepper, to taste. Pour the cheese sauce over the cauliflower and macaroni. Scatter the remaining cheese on top and bake for 20–25 minutes until golden brown.

Selections per serving:
1 Carbohydrate; 1/2 Fat; 1/2 Milk; 1 Protein; 1 Vegetable;
20 Optional Calories

Variation:
Replace half the cheese with 1 oz (30 g) of lean back bacon rashers, grilled until crisp, cut in strips and added at the end of step 2. This will reduce the Calories to 295 per serving and make it unsuitable for vegetarians.

Pasta Quills with Four Cheeses

Serves 2

Preparation time: 15 minutes
Cooking time: 15 minutes
Calories per serving: 500

Freezing not recommended

$\mathcal{V}$ **If using vegetarian cheese**

The *quattro formaggi* – or four cheeses – in this recipe are mozzarella, fontina, Gruyère and Edam, but as you need only a tiny sliver of each cheese, you may prefer to use just two of them. If you have difficulty finding fontina, use Edam or processed cheese slices instead.

4 oz (120 g) pasta quills (penne)
2 teaspoons margarine
2 teaspoons plain flour
7 fl oz (210 ml) skimmed milk
1 oz (30 g) mozzarella cheese, grated
1 oz (30 g) Gruyère cheese, grated
1 oz (30 g) fontina cheese, sliced thinly
1 oz (30 g) Edam cheese, sliced thinly
2 teaspoons grated parmesan cheese, to serve
salt and freshly ground black pepper

Cook's note:
Some supermarkets sell grated mozzarella cheese in re-sealable packs. These are perfect for storing in the freezer, allowing you to use small quantities when and as you need them.

Selections per serving:
2 Carbohydrate; 1 Fat; $1/4$ Milk; 2 Protein; 30 Optional Calories

Variations:
Use this recipe as the basis for a delicious Alfredo sauce. Simply replace all four cheeses with 3 oz (90 g) fresh grated parmesan cheese, and add 2 tablespoons of double cream to the sauce. This will reduce the Protein Selection to $1^1/2$ and add an extra 50 Optional Calories to the original recipe. The Calories per serving will increase to 550.

For a cheese and herb sauce, stir in 1 tablespoon each of freshly chopped parsley, basil, dill and chives just before serving.

1. Cook the pasta in plenty of lightly salted boiling water for 8–10 minutes or until just *al dente*.
2. Meanwhile, place the margarine, flour and milk in a small saucepan. Heat gently, whisking constantly until the mixture boils and thickens.
3. Remove the pan from the heat and add the mozzarella, Gruyère, fontina and Edam cheeses, stirring constantly until they have melted and the sauce is smooth. Season to taste with salt and plenty of black pepper.
4. Drain the cooked pasta and divide between 2 warm bowls. Pour on the cheese sauce and sprinkle each serving with 1 teaspoon of parmesan cheese. Serve immediately, offering extra ground black pepper separately.

Pasta with Fish

Fresh fish and shellfish are plentiful and economical in the Mediterranean, a fact which is reflected in the number of pasta recipes which feature seafood. In this chapter you will find fish salads, quick supper dishes (a few of which rely upon that good old store-cupboard standby – tuna fish), hearty bakes and gratins along with more delicate recipes which are perfect for entertaining.

Sea Shell Salad

Serves 4

Preparation and cooking time:
20 minutes
Calories per serving: 250

Freezing not recommended

This summer recipe is ideal for picnics and packed lunches, but do take care to keep it well chilled.

6 oz (180 g) small pasta shells (*conchiglie*)
5 fl oz (150 ml) low-fat natural yogurt
2 spring onions, chopped
½ red pepper, de-seeded and cut in matchsticks
2 teaspoons chopped fresh tarragon
2 teaspoons chopped fresh parsley
1 teaspoon lime juice
8 oz (240 g) cooked prawns, peeled
salt and freshly ground black pepper

1. Cook the pasta in plenty of lightly salted boiling water for 8–10 minutes until *al dente*. Rinse well with cold water and drain thoroughly.
2. In a large bowl, gently mix together the pasta, yogurt, spring onions, red pepper and herbs.
3. Sprinkle the lime juice over the prawns and fold them into the pasta salad. Season with salt and pepper. Chill well before serving.

Selections per serving:
1½ Carbohydrate; ¼ Milk; 1 Protein

Pasta with Tuna and Black Olives

Serves 2

Preparation and cooking time:
30 minutes
Calories per serving: 335

Freezing not recommended

Here is a satisfying recipe which can be rustled up in no time at all. Many of the ingredients will already be in your store-cupboard, so try out this recipe when your day has been too hectic to plan ahead.

2 teaspoons olive oil
1 small onion, chopped
1 garlic clove, chopped
10 small black olives, stoned
7 oz (210 g) canned chopped tomatoes
a pinch of dried thyme
a pinch of dried oregano
4 oz (120 g) pasta *lumache* (large pipe shapes)
4 oz (120 g) canned tuna fish in brine, drained
salt and freshly ground black pepper

1. Heat the olive oil in a small saucepan and gently cook the onion, garlic and olives until the onion is translucent. Stir in the tomatoes and the dried herbs. Bring to a boil, reduce the heat and simmer gently, uncovered, for 10 minutes.
2. Meanwhile, cook the pasta in plenty of lightly salted boiling water for 8–10 minutes, until *al dente*. Drain well.
3. Add the tuna fish to the sauce. Season with salt and pepper and simmer for 5 minutes more. Divide the pasta between 4 warm bowls, spoon the sauce over the top and serve immediately.

Cook's note:
Lumache is similar to macaroni, but larger and curved at one end – like a snail.

Selections per serving:
2 Carbohydrate; 1½ Fat; 1 Protein; 1½ Vegetable

Smoked Mackerel Salad

Serves 2

Preparation time: 15 minutes
Cooking time: 10 minutes
Calories per serving: 430

Freezing not recommended

2 oz (60 g) wholemeal pasta
 shapes (ie: twists or spirals)
1 teaspoon walnut or sunflower
 oil
1 medium dessert apple
2 tablespoons lemon juice
2 sticks celery
2-inch (5 cm) piece of
 cucumber

4 oz (120 g) smoked mackerel
 fillet, skinned
2 tablespoons chopped fresh
 parsley
1/2 oz (15 g) chopped walnuts,
 toasted
For the dressing:
21/2 fl oz (75 ml) low-fat natural
 yogurt
2 teaspoons horseradish relish
salt and freshly ground black
 pepper
mixed salad leaves, to serve

1. Cook the pasta in a large pan of lightly salted boiling water for about 10 minutes until it is just *al dente*. Drain well, rinse through with cold running water and drain again. Transfer the pasta to a large bowl and stir in the oil.
2. Core and slice the apple into small pieces and toss with the lemon juice in a bowl. Chop the celery, dice the cucumber and add both to the pasta.
3. Break the mackerel fillet into large flakes and carefully fold them into the pasta. Reserving the lemon juice, add the apple slices and half of the parsley.
4. Make the dressing by whisking together the yogurt, horseradish and reserved lemon juice. Season well with salt and pepper. Fold the dressing into the salad and divide it between 2 plates, sprinkling the nuts and remaining parsley on top. Serve with a few green salad leaves – young spinach, rocket or lamb's lettuce.

Cook's note:
Chill the salad before serving and eat it on the same day.

Selections per serving:
1 Carbohydrate; 1 Fat; 1/2 Fruit; 1/4 Milk; 2 Protein; 1/2 Vegetable;
20 Optional Calories

Melon and Prawn Salad

Serves 4

Preparation and cooking time:
30 minutes
Calories per serving: 285

Freezing not recommended

Use whatever melons are in season for this tasty seafood salad. Try charentais, ogen or cantaloupe.

6 oz (180 g) pasta shells
 (*conchiglie*)
8 oz (240 g) peeled prawns,
 thawed if frozen
1 seasonal melon, halved and

de-seeded
6 oz (180 g) cucumber, cut in
 chunks
2 tomatoes, skinned, de-seeded
 and cut in strips
4 large leaves of lollo rosso
 lettuce
a sprig of mint, to garnish
For the dressing:
4 teaspoons olive oil
zest and juice of 1/2 lemon
1 tablespoon fresh chopped
 mint
salt and freshly ground black
 pepper

1. Cook the pasta shells in a pan of lightly salted boiling water for about 8 minutes or until just tender. Drain and rinse under cold running water and drain again. Place in a large bowl.
2. Add the prawns to the pasta. Use a melon baller or cut the melon into cubes. Add the melon, cucumber and tomatoes to the pasta. Tear the lettuce into pieces and carefully fold it in.
3. Make the dressing by whisking all the ingredients together. Pour it over the salad and toss gently. Divide between 4 plates, garnish with sprigs of mint and serve immediately.

Cook's note:
If you are preparing this dish ahead, refrigerate the salad and dressing separately and toss together just before serving.

Selections per serving:
11/2 Carbohydrate; 1 Fat; 1/2 Fruit; 1 Protein; 1 Vegetable

Haddock and Broccoli Lasagne

Serves 4

Preparation time: 25 minutes

Calories per serving: 420

Cooking time: 35 minutes

Freezing recommended

Lasagne comes from the Greek *lasanou* and the Roman *laganum*. These were the earliest known forms of pasta and were fried or roasted.

1¼ lb (600 g) fresh haddock fillet, skinned
1 bay leaf
1 small onion, quartered
1 garlic clove
4 tablespoons dry white wine
4 oz (120 g) leeks, sliced thickly
8 oz (240 g) broccoli, cut into small florets
½ pint (300 ml) skimmed milk
1 tablespoon margarine
2 oz (60 g) plain flour
1 tablespoon chopped fresh dill
4 oz (120 g) (6 sheets) no pre-cook lasagne
2 oz (60 g) Cheddar or Gruyère cheese, grated
salt and freshly ground black pepper
lemon slices and fresh dill, to garnish

1. Place the haddock fillet in a large shallow frying pan and add just enough water to cover. Add the bay leaf, onion, garlic clove and wine. Season with salt and pepper. Bring to a boil and then simmer for 5 minutes or until tender.
2. Using a slotted spoon, transfer the fish on to a plate and flake, discarding any bones. Strain and reserve the poaching juices.
3. Preheat the oven to Gas Mark 5/190°C/375°F.
4. Cook the leeks and broccoli in lightly salted boiling water for 5–8 minutes until the broccoli is just tender. Drain and refresh the vegetables under cold running water.

5. Combine the milk and the strained poaching juices in a measuring jug, bringing the level to 1 pint (600 ml), adding water if necessary. Transfer to a small saucepan, add the margarine and flour and heat, whisking constantly, until the sauce boils and thickens. Remove from the heat and season with salt and pepper. Stir in the chopped dill.
6. Pour a third of the sauce into a shallow, ovenproof serving dish. Spoon in half of the haddock, leeks and broccoli and cover with 3 lasagne sheets. Pour over another third of the sauce, and add the remaining fish and vegetables. Layer three more lasagne sheets and top with the remaining sauce, spreading it out to reach the edges.
7. Sprinkle with the grated cheese, cover with foil and bake for 20 minutes. Remove the foil and bake for 15 minutes more, until golden brown.
8. Garnish with lemon slices and fresh dill and serve immediately.

Selections per serving:
1½ Carbohydrate; ½ Fat; ¼ Milk; 2½ Protein; 1 Vegetable; 25 Optional Calories

Variation:
Add sliced mushrooms in place of some of the broccoli, or replace 4 oz (120 g) haddock with 4 oz (120 g) peeled prawns or 2 hard boiled eggs, chopped. Using prawns will increase the Calories to 430 per serving and using eggs will bring them to 450 per serving.

Pasta Salad Niçoise

Serves 4

Preparation time: 20 minutes
Cooking time: 10 minutes
Calories per serving: 365

Freezing not recommended

1 teaspoon salt
4 oz (120 g) pasta shapes
(ie: quills)
2 eggs
6 oz (180 g) frozen haricot
beans, halved
1 red pepper, de-seeded and
sliced finely
4-inch (10 cm) piece cucumber,
diced
6 spring onions, trimmed and
cut in ½-inch (1 cm) lengths

12 cherry tomatoes, halved
6 large black olives, stoned and
halved or 10 small olives
2 tablespoons chopped fresh
parsley
7 oz (210 g) canned tuna fish in
brine, drained
2 oz (60 g) canned anchovy
fillets, drained, rinsed and
cut in strips
For the dressing:
4 teaspoons olive oil
1 tablespoon red wine vinegar
1 tablespoon lemon juice
¼ teaspoon Dijon mustard
salt and freshly ground black
pepper

1. Bring a large pan of water to a boil, add 1 teaspoon of salt and
the pasta and bring back to a boil. Cook for 2 minutes and add the
whole eggs for hard-boiling. Boil for 3 minutes more and then add
the beans. Bring back to a boil for about 3 minutes more or until
the pasta is just tender. Drain the pasta, eggs and beans together in
a large colander and rinse them thoroughly with cold running water
until all are cold.
2. Put the pasta and beans in a large serving bowl. Add the red
pepper, cucumber, spring onions, tomatoes, olives and half of
the parsley.
3. Break the tuna fish into large flakes. Whisk together the dressing
ingredients in a cup and pour over the salad, folding it in carefully
with the tuna so as not to break up the fish. Divide the salad
between 4 plates.
4. Shell the eggs and quarter them. Arrange 2 sections on top of
each serving. Divide the anchovy strips between the four salads and
arrange them in a criss-cross pattern. Sprinkle with the rest of the
parsley and serve chilled.

Selections per serving:
1 Carbohydrate; 1 Fat; 1½ Protein; 1½ Vegetable; 35 Optional
Calories

Spaghetti Marinara

Serves 2

Preparation and cooking time:
30 minutes
Calories per serving: 350

**Freezing recommended
(sauce only)**

**An authentic marinara sauce
is simply made of tomatoes
and garlic, slow-cooked to
a thick rich sauce. Many
versions, however, include a
mixture of seafood, and as
marinara also describes the
workday uniform worn by
ordinary seamen, the con-
nection doesn't seem so fishy!**

2 teaspoons olive oil
1 small onion, chopped
1 garlic clove, chopped
7 oz (210 g) canned chopped
tomatoes
2 tablespoons chopped fresh
parsley
2 tablespoons fresh basil,
shredded
4 oz (120 g) spaghetti
2 oz (60 g) peeled prawns
2 oz (60 g) canned tuna fish in
brine, drained
2 oz (60 g) frozen cooked
mussels, thawed
salt and freshly ground black
pepper
chopped parsley, to garnish

1. Heat the oil in a medium-size saucepan and gently cook the onion
and garlic for 5 minutes until the onion becomes translucent. Add
the tomatoes and fresh herbs and simmer, uncovered, for
15–20 minutes or until the sauce has reduced and thickened.
2. Meanwhile, cook the spaghetti in plenty of lightly salted boiling
water for 8–10 minutes, until *al dente*.
3. Season the tomato sauce with salt and pepper. Stir in the
prawns, tuna fish and mussels, and heat through for 5 minutes.
4. Drain the cooked spaghetti and divide between 2 warm bowls.
Spoon the marinara sauce over the pasta and garnish with the
chopped parsley. Serve immediately.

Cook's note:
Make the most of canned seafoods (eg: clams, mussels and prawns)
as they work extremely well in this recipe.

Selections per serving:
2 Carbohydrate; 1 Fat; 1½ Protein; 2 Vegetable

Variations:
Clams and squid rings are also delicious in this sauce.

Bucatini with Tuna and Tomato

Serves 4

Preparation and cooking time:
30 minutes

**Freezing recommended
(sauce only)**

Butta la pasta – **throw in the
pasta! Most sauces can be
made well in advance, but
pasta has to receive last
minute attention. Leaving the
office, Italian men would ring
home with this command, as
a signal that they'd want their
lunch soon. Thankfully, times
have changed!**

4 teaspoons olive oil
1 onion, chopped
2 garlic cloves, chopped
14 oz (420 g) canned chopped
    tomatoes
6 tablespoons dry white wine
7 oz (210 g) canned tuna fish,
    in brine, drained and flaked
2 tablespoons chopped capers
8 oz (240 g) *bucatini* or
    spaghetti
salt and freshly ground black
    pepper
2 tablespoons chopped fresh
    parsley, to garnish

1. Heat the oil in a saucepan and sauté the onion and garlic for
5 minutes over a medium heat, until softened.
2. Add the chopped tomatoes and wine. Season with salt and
pepper. Bring to a boil, reduce the heat and simmer, uncovered,
for 10 minutes, stirring occasionally.
3. Add the flaked tuna fish and capers and cook gently for
10 minutes more.
4. Meanwhile, cook the pasta in plenty of lightly salted boiling
water for 8–10 minutes, until *al dente*. Drain thoroughly and
divide between 4 warm plates.
5. Spoon the sauce over the pasta. Sprinkle with the parsley and
serve at once.

Selections per serving:
2 Carbohydrate; 1 Fat; ½ Protein; 1½ Vegetable; 40 Optional
Calories

Calories per serving: 325

Variation:
Replace 1 oz (30 g) of tuna fish with ½ oz (15 g) of chopped
anchovy fillets.

Pasta with Sun-dried Tomato and Prawn Sauce

Serves 2

Preparation and cooking time:
25 minutes
Calories per serving: 315

Freezing not recommended

**Taglierini is a very fine,
ribbon-like pasta, available
in spinach, egg or tomato
varieties and is the perfect
pasta to enjoy with this
delicate pink sauce.**

1 tablespoon sun-dried tomato
    paste
1 garlic clove, crushed
3 tablespoons dry white wine
2 oz (60 g) cooked peeled
    prawns
2 oz (60 g) low-fat soft cheese
4 oz (120 g) taglierini,
    spaghettini or spaghetti
salt and freshly ground black
    pepper
fresh basil leaves, to garnish

1. Place the tomato paste, garlic, white wine and prawns in a small
saucepan. Heat gently for 10 minutes, stirring occasionally.
2. Transfer the prawn mixture to a food processor. Add the soft
cheese, and blend until smooth. Season with salt and pepper. Pour
the sauce back into the rinsed saucepan and warm through over a
very low heat. Do not allow the sauce to boil.
3. Meanwhile, cook the pasta in plenty of lightly salted boiling
water for 5–7 minutes, or until *al dente*. Drain and divide between
2 warm bowls.
4. Spoon the prawn sauce over the pasta. Garnish with fresh basil
and serve immediately.

Cook's note:
You can use 2 teaspoons of tomato purée instead of the sun-dried
tomato paste: the flavour will not be as intense but there will be no
½ Fat Selection.

Selections per serving:
2 Carbohydrate; ½ Fat; 1 Protein; 20 Optional Calories

Tagliatelle with Cod, Chive and Parsley Sauce

Serves 4

Preparation time: 10 minutes
Cooking time: 25 minutes
Calories per serving: 415

Freezing not recommended

4 teaspoons margarine
4 teaspoons fresh white breadcrumbs
1¼ lb (600 g) skinned and boned cod fillet
1 pint (600 ml) skimmed milk
1 bay leaf
2 tablespoons cornflour, blended with a little water
8 oz (240 g) spinach tagliatelle
2 tablespoons chopped fresh parsley
2 tablespoons snipped fresh chives
2 teaspoons lemon juice
1 teaspoon finely grated lemon zest
salt and freshly ground black pepper

1. Melt the margarine in a large saucepan and sauté the fresh breadcrumbs until they are golden and crisp. Transfer the crumbs to a small bowl and wipe the saucepan clean with kitchen paper.
2. Place the fish in the saucepan and add the milk and bay leaf. Season with a little salt and pepper and heat gently, poaching the fish for 8–10 minutes until cooked. (The fish should be opaque and flake easily when ready). Discard the bay leaf.
3. Carefully lift the fish on to a plate. Cover with foil and keep warm. Stir the blended cornflour into the saucepan. Heat, stirring constantly, until the sauce boils and thickens. Reduce the heat and cook gently for 2 minutes more.
4. Cook the tagliatelle in a large pan of lightly salted boiling water for 8–10 minutes until *al dente*. Meanwhile, stir the parsley and chives into the white sauce. Add the lemon juice and adjust the seasoning to taste. Gently separate the fish into large flakes, and divide into four portions. Mix the lemon zest into the golden breadcrumbs.
5. Drain the tagliatelle and fold into the parsley and chive sauce. Divide evenly between 4 warm plates. Gently spoon the fish portions on to each serving. Scatter the lemony breadcrumbs on top and serve immediately.

Selections per serving:
2 Carbohydrate; 1 Fat; ½ Milk; 2 Protein; 25 Optional Calories

Variation:
Replace the chives and parsley with tarragon or dill for a very different flavour.

Rigatoni with Seafood Sauce

Serves 4

Preparation and cooking time: 20 minutes
Calories per serving: 340

Freezing not recommended

Next time you are in an Italian restaurant look out for the term *pasta asciutta* on the menu; this literally means 'dried pasta' but actually refers to the way it is served – with just enough sauce to moisten the pasta.

8 oz (240 g) rigatoni or quill pasta
4 teaspoons olive oil
1 garlic clove, chopped finely
1 small red chilli pepper, de-seeded and chopped finely
8 oz (240 g) ready prepared mixed seafood (ie: squid, mussels, prawns)
4 oz (120 g) cooked white crab meat (fresh, frozen or canned)
4 large tomatoes, peeled, de-seeded and chopped finely
4 tablespoons dry white wine
1 tablespoon chopped fresh parsley
salt and freshly ground black pepper

1. Cook the pasta in a saucepan of lightly salted boiling water for 8–10 minutes or until just *al dente*.
2. Meanwhile, heat the oil in a saucepan and gently sauté the garlic and chilli until the garlic just begins to brown. Add the prepared seafood, crab, tomatoes and white wine and heat until just boiling. Cook briskly for 3–5 minutes, stirring occasionally (some of the wine will evaporate).
3. Season with salt and pepper, reduce the heat and keep the mixture warm.
4. Drain the cooked pasta and divide between 4 warm bowls. Spoon the fish on to the pasta. Sprinkle with the chopped parsley and serve immediately.

Cook's note:
Look out for the chilled packs of ready prepared and cooked mixed seafood in your local supermarket.

Selections per serving:
2 Carbohydrate; 1 Fat; 1½ Protein; 1 Vegetable; 15 Optional Calories

Tagliatelle with Smoked Salmon and Asparagus

Serves 4

Preparation and cooking time: 25 minutes
Calories per serving: 355

Freezing not recommended

Delicate sauces require flat ribbon-like pasta to allow just the right amount of sauce to coat the pasta. Use tagliatelle or linguine in this recipe.

4 oz (120 g) low-fat soft cheese
6 oz (180 g) smoked salmon trimmings
4 tablespoons dry white wine
1 teaspoon lemon juice
1 tablespoon chopped dill
12 oz (360 g) fresh asparagus, trimmed and cut in 2-inch (5 cm) pieces
8 oz (240 g) fresh tagliatelle or linguine
salt and freshly ground black pepper
fresh dill sprigs, to garnish

1. Put the soft cheese, 2 oz (60 g) of the salmon trimmings, the wine and lemon juice into a liquidiser and process until smooth. Transfer to a small saucepan and heat through very gently. Do not allow the sauce to boil. Season with salt and pepper and stir in the chopped dill and remaining salmon trimmings.
2. Cook the asparagus in lightly salted boiling water for 5 minutes until just tender. Drain.
3. Cook the pasta in plenty of lightly salted boiling water for 2–3 minutes until *al dente*. Drain thoroughly and return the pasta to the warm saucepan. Add the sauce, the remaining salmon trimmings and the asparagus, carefully folding them together. Divide the tagliatelle between 4 warm plates and garnish with a piece of fresh dill. Serve immediately.

Cook's note:
Ask for smoked salmon trimmings at the deli counter of your supermarket; they are much cheaper than the slices!

Selections per serving:
2 Carbohydrate; 2 Protein; 1 Vegetable; 15 Optional Calories

Variation:
Replace the asparagus with mange tout, tiny broccoli florets or courgette matchsticks.

Baked Italian Fish Casserole

Serves 4

Preparation time: 10 minutes
Cooking time: 40 minutes
Calories per serving: 375

Freezing not recommended

Use the freshest, firm white fish available – cod, haddock or hake are equally well-suited for this tasty supper dish.

6 oz (180 g) macaroni, fusilli or pasta shells
1 tablespoon margarine
1 garlic clove, chopped
1 small onion, chopped
8 oz (240 g) frozen spinach, thawed
1 tablespoon plain flour
14 oz (420 g) canned chopped tomatoes
1/4 pint (150 ml) skimmed milk
1 tablespoon chopped fresh oregano
1 lb (480 g) skinned and boned haddock, cut into chunks
1 oz (30 g) fresh white breadcrumbs
1 tablespoon parmesan cheese, grated
salt and freshly ground black pepper

1. Preheat the oven to Gas Mark 5/190°C/375°F. Cook the pasta in plenty of boiling salted water for 8–10 minutes or until just *al dente*. Drain.
2. Melt the margarine in a saucepan and gently cook the garlic and onion until softened but not browned. Add the spinach and cook for 5 minutes more.
3. Sprinkle in the flour and gradually add the tomatoes, milk and oregano. Bring to a boil, stirring constantly, until the sauce thickens. Season with salt and pepper.
4. Carefully fold the pasta and fish into the sauce. Spoon into an ovenproof gratin dish. Mix together the breadcrumbs and cheese and sprinkle evenly over the surface. Bake for approximately 20 minutes or until golden brown.

Selections per serving:
1 1/2 Carbohydrate; 1/2 Fat; 1 1/2 Protein; 2 Vegetable; 55 Optional Calories

Salmon and Pasta Bake

Serves 4

Preparation time: 20 minutes
Cooking time: 20 minutes
Calories per serving: 380

Freezing not recommended

2 oz (60 g) *conchiglie* (pasta shells)
1 pint (600 ml) skimmed milk
2 oz (60 g) plain flour
1 tablespoon margarine

1 teaspoon Dijon mustard
3 oz (90 g) Gruyère or mozzarella cheese, grated
2 teaspoons chopped fresh dill
7 oz (210 g) canned salmon, drained and flaked
1 oz (30 g) fresh white breadcrumbs
salt and freshly ground black pepper

1. Preheat the oven to Gas Mark 5/190°C/375°F.
2. Cook the pasta shells in plenty of lightly salted boiling water for 8–10 minutes, or until *al dente*. Drain well and set aside.
3. Gently heat the milk, flour and margarine in a small saucepan, stirring constantly with a wire whisk, until thickened and smooth. Remove from the heat and stir in the mustard and 2 oz (60 g) of the cheese. Add the dill and season with salt and pepper.
4. Arrange the cooked pasta shells and the salmon in 1 large or 4 individual ovenproof gratin dishes. Pour the sauce over and stir to coat.
5. Mix the remaining cheese together with the breadcrumbs and sprinkle evenly over the surface. Bake for approximately 20 minutes, or until golden brown.

Selections per serving:
1 Carbohydrate; 1/2 Fat; 1/2 Milk; 2 1/2 Protein; 30 Optional Calories

Pasta and Monkfish 'en Papillote'

Serves 4

Preparation time: 10 minutes
Cooking time: 40 minutes
Calories per serving: 290

Freezing not recommended

Tricolour fusilli or *eliche* (twists) are the ideal shapes and colour for this delicious recipe. If entertaining, let your guests open the parcels at the table so that the element of surprise and wonderful aroma can be savoured! Serve with fresh green vegetables.

2 oz (60 g) dried pasta shapes (ie: twists or quills)

1 oz (30 g) lean back bacon rashers
2 teaspoons olive oil
1 garlic clove (optional)
2 oz (60 g) small button mushrooms, sliced
1 small red or yellow pepper, de-seeded and sliced
2 teaspoons chopped fresh parsley
2 teaspoons snipped fresh chives
3 tablespoons dry white wine
4 tablespoons double cream
10 oz (300 g) monkfish tail, cut in chunks
salt and freshly ground black pepper

1. Preheat the oven to Gas Mark 5/190°C/375°F.
2. Cook the pasta in plenty of lightly salted boiling water for 8–10 minutes, until *al dente*. Drain thoroughly.
3. Meanwhile, trim the bacon of any visible fat.
4. Heat the oil in a non-stick frying pan and sauté the garlic clove, if using, along with the bacon, mushrooms and pepper for 4–5 minutes. Discard the garlic clove and stir in the chopped herbs, white wine, and cream. Heat through gently.
5. Divide the cooked pasta and the monkfish between 4 large sheets of greaseproof paper or cooking foil. Spoon the vegetable and bacon sauce over the pasta and fish and season with salt and pepper.
6. Fold the parcels up, sealing them well to prevent any steam from escaping. Place them in a large shallow baking tray and cook for 15–20 minutes, until the fish is tender. Serve immediately.

Selections per serving:
1/2 Carbohydrate; 1/2 Fat; 1 1/2 Protein; 1/2 Vegetable; 60 Optional Calories

Variation:
Experiment with different fish and vegetables – try using prawns or tuna steaks and add oregano or thyme for a Mediterranean flavour.

Pasta with Meat and Poultry

Once the staple diet of peasants and farmers, pasta is one of the most popular, healthy and versatile of foods to enjoy with meat, poultry and offal. ⚒ Traditionally, pasta was used to eke out a family's preserved meats – sausages, salamis and hams – but these days we are encouraged to reduce our intake of meats and increase our carbohydrate consumption to benefit our health and well-being rather than our purses! ⚒ Robust meat sauces go well with short, heavy pasta shapes – fusilli, penne, rigatoni or shells – which trap meat in their folds and hollows. And, of course, lasagne sheets can be layered or rolled into tubes and filled with savoury sauces. The variations are endless – consider using pasta instead of rice in some of your own favourite Weight Watchers recipes.

Vermicelli with Crispy Bacon and Chives

Serves 2

Preparation and cooking time:
20 minutes
Calories per serving: 325

Freezing not recommended

Vermicelli means 'little worms'! Finer than spaghettini, it is particularly good with very light sauces. Also look out for *capellini* ('fine hair') and *capelli d'angelo* ('angel's hair'), which is finer still. These can all be used in this, or similar recipes.

2 oz (60 g) lean, smoked back bacon rashers
4 oz (120 g) vermicelli
2 tablespoons fresh snipped chives
1 oz (30 g) parmesan cheese, grated
freshly ground black pepper

1. Grill the bacon rashers until brown and very crisp. Crumble on to kitchen paper and reserve.
2. Cook the pasta in plenty of lightly salted boiling water for 6–8 minutes until *al dente*. Drain well and transfer to a warm bowl.
3. Add the bacon, chives and grated cheese to the pasta, and season with black pepper. Toss together until the cheese begins to melt. Divide between 2 warm bowls and serve immediately.

Cook's note:
Serve this speedy pasta dish with a tomato and basil salad or steamed broccoli or spinach.

Selections per serving:
2 Carbohydrate; 2 Protein; 30 Optional Calories

Pepperoni Pasta

Serves 2

Preparation and cooking time:
30 minutes
Calories per serving: 450

Freezing not recommended

Salami originates from the Grecian town Salamis and is widely available, with endless varieties.

Pepperoni is a mix of ground pork and beef flavoured with paprika or cayenne pepper.

2 teaspoons vegetable oil
1 onion, sliced
2 small carrots, sliced thinly
1 small green pepper, de-seeded and sliced
7 oz (210 g) canned chopped tomatoes
1 tablespoon tomato purée
1 teaspoon brown sugar
1 teaspoon paprika
4 oz (120 g) pepperoni or garlic sausage, sliced finely
4 oz (120 g) pasta shapes (ie: twists or quills)
salt and freshly ground black pepper
parsley, to garnish

1. Heat the oil in a small saucepan and gently cook the onion and carrots for 4–5 minutes. Stir in the green pepper, chopped tomatoes, purée, sugar, paprika and pepperoni. Cover and simmer for 10–15 minutes or until the vegetables are tender.
2. Meanwhile, cook the pasta in plenty of lightly salted boiling water for 8–10 minutes until *al dente*. Drain and toss into the sauce.
3. Divide on to 2 warm plates and serve, garnished with sprigs of parsley.

Selections per serving:
2 Carbohydrate; 1 Fat; 2 Protein; 1 Vegetable; 10 Optional Calories

Tomato Pasta with Sausage

Serves 4

Preparation and cooking time:
35 minutes
Calories per serving: 440

Freezing not recommended

Use a tomato flavoured pasta for this tasty (and very Italian) way with the humble sausage. Buy the best quality pork sausage you can find.

2 teaspoons vegetable oil
1 small onion, chopped
1 garlic clove, crushed

8 oz (240 g) thick pork sausages (approx 4)
4 oz (120 g) small button mushrooms, wiped
2 teaspoons chopped fresh rosemary
4 fl oz (120 ml) dry white wine
8 oz (240 g) tomato flavoured pasta (ie: twists or *orechiette*)
a pinch of freshly grated nutmeg
2 oz (60 g) mozzarella cheese, grated
salt and freshly ground black pepper

1. Heat the oil and gently cook the onion and garlic for 5–8 minutes until softened and golden.
2. Remove the skin from the sausages and roughly break up the meat. Add it to the pan and cook for 5 minutes more, breaking up and turning the sausage meat until well browned.
3. Add the mushrooms, rosemary and wine, reduce the heat and simmer for 10 minutes. Meanwhile, cook the pasta in plenty of lightly salted boiling water for 8–10 minutes until *al dente*. Drain.
4. Season the sausage mixture with the nutmeg, salt and pepper. Stir in the drained hot pasta and divide between 4 warm bowls. Sprinkle the mozzarella cheese on top and serve immediately.

Cook's note:
If you enjoy the flavour of garlic but do not want it to dominate a recipe, add a whole clove and discard it before serving.

Selections per serving:
2 Carbohydrate; ½ Fat; 2 Protein; ½ Vegetable; 25 Optional Calories

Chicken Liver and Mushroom Medley

Serves 2

Preparation and cooking time:
30 minutes
Calories per serving: 420

Freezing not recommended

½ oz (15 g) lean back bacon rasher
4 oz (120 g) pasta shapes (ie: macaroni or spirals)
2 teaspoons vegetable oil
1 onion, sliced
4 oz (120 g) chicken livers, sliced
½ teaspoon hot chilli powder
7 oz (210 g) canned chopped tomatoes, drained

2 oz (60 g) button mushrooms, sliced
1 tablespoon tomato purée
4 tablespoons red wine or medium sherry
1 teaspoon fresh chopped thyme or rosemary
1 teaspoon Worcestershire sauce
6 tablespoons low-fat natural yogurt
salt and freshly ground black pepper
chopped parsley, to garnish

1. Trim the bacon of any visible fat and cut in strips.
2. Cook the pasta in plenty of lightly salted boiling water for 8–10 minutes until *al dente*.
3. Heat the oil in a saucepan and sauté the onion until it is lightly browned and softened. Stir in the bacon and chicken livers, sprinkle in the chilli powder and cook for 3–4 minutes.
4. Add the tomatoes, mushrooms, purée, wine or sherry, herbs and Worcestershire sauce and simmer, uncovered, for 5 minutes more.
5. Meanwhile, drain the pasta thoroughly and divide between 4 warm plates. Remove the sauce from the heat. Season with salt and pepper and swirl in the yogurt. Spoon the sauce over the pasta and sprinkle liberally with chopped parsley.

Cook's note:
Chicken livers are generally sold frozen. Once thawed, wash and dry them thoroughly before use, and cut away any sinewy or green-tinged liver, which has a bitter taste.

Selections per serving:
2 Carbohydrate; 1 Fat; 2 Protein; 2 Vegetable; 55 Optional Calories

Spicy Chicken and Pasta with Apricots

Serves 4

Preparation time: 15 minutes
Cooking time: 20 minutes
Calories per serving: 325

Freezing not recommended

Leaf coriander is a member of the carrot family and is native to the Mediterranean. In Italy it is known as *cilantro*.

Always use some of the stem as this is full of flavour.

4 teaspoons vegetable oil
1 onion, sliced
1 lb (480 g) boneless chicken breast, cut into strips
2 tablespoons mild curry powder
1 teaspoon finely chopped root ginger
³/4 pint (450 ml) chicken stock
2 oz (60 g) ready-to-eat dried apricots, chopped
4 oz (120 g) small wholemeal pasta shapes (ie: shells)
4 tablespoons low-fat natural yogurt
2 tablespoons chopped coriander
salt and freshly ground black pepper

1. Heat the oil in a large frying pan. Sauté the onion for 5–8 minutes until softened and golden, stirring frequently.
2. Add the chicken, curry powder and ginger to the pan and stir-fry over a moderate heat for 2–3 minutes. Stir in the chicken stock and bring to a boil.
3. Reduce the heat and add the apricots and pasta shapes. Season with salt and pepper. Cover and simmer gently for 20 minutes until the chicken and pasta are tender.
4. Remove from the heat and stir in the yogurt and chopped coriander. Serve immediately.

Selections per serving:
1 Carbohydrate; 1 Fat; ¹/2 Fruit; 3 Protein; ¹/4 Vegetable; 10 Optional Calories

Variation:
Stir in ¹/2 oz (15 g) of ground almonds during step 3. This would increase the Optional Calories to 25 per serving and the Calories per serving to 335.

Huntsman Chicken

Serves 4

Preparation time: 10 minutes
Cooking time: 40–45 minutes
Calories per serving: 350

Freezing recommended (sauce only, after step 2)

11 oz (330 g) skinless, boneless chicken breast
2 teaspoons olive oil
1 onion, sliced
1 garlic clove, crushed
4 fl oz (120 ml) dry white wine
1 chicken stock cube
13 oz (390 g) canned red tomato passata
1 teaspoon fresh basil, shredded
1 teaspoon white sugar
6 oz (180 g) pappardelle or tagliatelle
1 oz (30 g) anchovy fillets in olive oil, rinsed and drained
12 large black olives
salt and freshly ground black pepper
2 tablespoons chopped fresh parsley, to serve

1. Cut the chicken in thumb-width strips and season well. Heat the oil in a pan and brown the chicken for a few minutes. Remove the chicken and set aside. Add the onion and the garlic to the pan and cook for 5 minutes. Pour in the wine and continue to cook until the wine has reduced by half.
2. Crumble the stock cube into the pan, add the passata, basil, sugar and chicken strips, and simmer over a low heat for 20 minutes or until the sauce has reduced and thickened a little.
3. Meanwhile, cook the pasta in plenty of lightly salted boiling water for approximately 6–8 minutes or until *al dente*.
4. Cut the anchovy fillets in strips. Add the anchovies and black olives to the chicken and simmer for 5 minutes more. Adjust the seasoning, if necessary.
5. Arrange the pasta on 4 plates. Spoon the chicken and sauce on top, leaving some of the pasta showing. Sprinkle the parsley in a line down the middle of the chicken and serve immediately.

Selections per serving:
1¹/2 Carbohydrate; 1 Fat; 2¹/2 Protein; 1 Vegetable; 35 Optional Calories

Variation:
Use sheets of spinach lasagne (verdi), cut lengthways once cooked.

Gammon and Pasta Toss

Serves 4

Preparation time: 20 minutes
+ 6 hours chilling
Cooking time: 10 minutes
Calories per serving: 420

Freezing not recommended

12 oz (360 g) lean gammon,
  cut in strips
2 large onions, sliced finely
8 fl oz (240 ml) unsweetened
  apple juice
1 tablespoon wholegrain
  mustard
1 garlic clove, crushed
4 oz (120 g) whole baby carrots
  or carrots cut in matchsticks
4 oz (120 g) green beans, halved
4 oz (120 g) pasta shapes
  (ie: *farfalle*, macaroni)
4 teaspoons vegetable oil
1 medium crisp dessert apple,
  peeled, cored and sliced
  thickly
2 teaspoons chopped fresh sage
4 tablespoons crème fraîche
salt and freshly ground black
  pepper

1. Place the gammon strips, onions, apple juice, mustard and garlic in a bowl. Mix well, cover and leave in the refrigerator to marinate for 6 hours or overnight.
2. Blanch the carrots and beans in lightly salted boiling water for 5–8 minutes or until just tender. Rinse well with cold running water, drain thoroughly and set aside to cool.
3. Cook the pasta in plenty of lightly salted boiling water for 8–10 minutes or until *al dente*. Drain well.
4. Drain the gammon and onion from the apple juice, reserving the marinade. Heat the oil in a large frying pan or wok and stir-fry the gammon and onion for 4–5 minutes until lightly browned.
5. Stir in the carrots, beans, pasta, apple and sage, the reserved marinade and salt and pepper to taste. Bring to a boil, then simmer for 3–4 minutes, stirring occasionally.
6. Stir in the crème fraîche and serve immediately.

Cook's note:
Steps 1–3 can be prepared up to 24 hours in advance.

Selections per serving:
1 Carbohydrate; 1 Fat; ½ Fruit; 2½ Protein; 1 Vegetable;
65 Optional Calories

Pork and Pasta Paprika

Serves 4

Preparation time: 10 minutes
Cooking time: 35–40 minutes
Calories per serving: 380

Freezing recommended

8 oz (240 g) pork fillet
2 teaspoons olive oil
1 onion, sliced finely
1 green pepper, de-seeded and
  sliced
2 garlic cloves, crushed
1 red or green chilli, chopped
  finely
1 tablespoon paprika
½ teaspoon caraway seeds or
  1 teaspoon cumin seeds
  (optional)
14 oz (420 g) canned passata
  (sieved tomatoes)
1¾ pints (1 litre) chicken stock
14 oz (420 g) canned cannellini
  beans, rinsed and drained
6 oz (180 g) wholewheat pasta
  spirals
5 tablespoons chopped fresh
  parsley
4 tablespoons low-fat natural
  yogurt
salt and freshly ground black
  pepper

1. Trim the pork fillet, and cut in ½-inch (1 cm) cubes.
2. Heat the oil in a very large pan and sauté the onion, pepper, garlic and chilli over a medium heat for 5 minutes until softened.
3. Add the pork, sprinkle the paprika and caraway or cumin seeds in and stir well to mix.
4. Spoon in the passata and stock and bring to a boil, then add the beans, pasta spirals, pork and 3 tablespoons of the parsley. Season with salt and pepper and stir well. Cook, uncovered, over a medium heat for 20–25 minutes until the pasta is tender and the sauce has thickened. (Add a little water if the sauce thickens too much.)
5. Spoon into a hot serving dish and swirl the yogurt on top. Sprinkle with the remaining parsley and a little paprika.

Selections per serving:
1½ Carbohydrate; ½ Fat; 2½ Protein; 1½ Vegetable; 20 Optional Calories

Beef Cannelloni

Serves 4

Preparation time: 10–15 minutes
Cooking time: 45 minutes
Calories per serving: 355

Freezing recommended

8 oz (240 g) lean minced beef
1 teaspoon olive oil
1 onion, chopped finely
2 garlic cloves, crushed
4 oz (120 g) mushrooms chopped finely
14 oz (420 g) canned plum tomatoes, drained with juice reserved
1 beef stock cube
1 teaspoon ground cinnamon
6 oz (180 g) (8 sheets) lasagne
4 oz (120 g) mozzarella cheese, drained and sliced
salt and freshly ground black pepper

1. Sauté the mince in a non-stick frying pan for about 5 minutes. Drain off any fat and set the meat aside.
2. Heat the oil and cook the onion and garlic over a medium heat for about 4 minutes until softened. Stir in the mushrooms and add the minced beef and the drained tomatoes. Crumble in the stock cube with the cinnamon, salt and freshly ground black pepper. Bring to a boil then reduce the heat and simmer, breaking down the tomatoes a little, for 20 minutes or until the liquid has been absorbed.
3. Preheat the oven to Gas Mark 5/190°C/375°F. Parboil the lasagne in a large pan of lightly salted boiling water for about 5 minutes until just tender. Rinse in cold water, drain and pat dry with kitchen paper. Lay the sheets of lasagne on the work surface and divide the beef mixture between them, spooning it down the middle of each sheet. Roll the sheets up from the long side and pack them snugly, seamside down, into a very lightly oiled ovenproof dish.
4. Spoon the reserved tomato juice around the pasta rolls and arrange the mozzarella cheese on top with a little more cinnamon if desired. Bake for 30 minutes until golden brown.

Cook's note:
You can use 8 cannelloni tubes instead of lasagne sheets but they are not as easy to fill!

Selections per serving:
1½ Carbohydrate; 2½ Protein; 1½ Vegetable; 15 Optional Calories

Boston Beef and Baked Bean Hotpot

Serves 4

Preparation time: 15 minutes
Cooking time: 40 minutes
Calories per serving: 350

Freezing recommended

President Jefferson (1743-1826) is thought to have introduced pasta to the Americans after visiting Italy.

This quick and tasty recipe will be a firm favourite to share with the children!

12 oz (360 g) extra lean minced beef
2 teaspoons vegetable oil
2 onions, chopped
½ pint (300 ml) beef stock
8 oz (240 g) canned plum tomatoes
15 oz (450 g) canned baked beans
4 oz (120 g) pasta shapes, ie: spirals
2 teaspoons Worcestershire sauce
2 teaspoons tomato purée
2 teaspoons barbecue sauce
a pinch of dried herbs
salt and freshly ground black pepper
chopped parsley, to garnish

1. Sauté the minced beef in a non-stick pan for 4–5 minutes, until browned. Drain off the fat.
2. Heat the oil in a large saucepan and gently cook the onions until soft and transparent. Stir in the browned mince along with the remaining ingredients, except for the parsley. Bring to a boil, reduce the heat and simmer, covered, for 40 minutes until the meat and pasta are cooked and tender.
3. Adjust the seasoning, if necessary, sprinkle liberally with fresh chopped parsley and serve.

Selections per serving:
2 Carbohydrate; ½ Fat; 2½ Protein; 1 Vegetable; 20 Optional Calories

Meatballs with Spaghetti in Sweet and Sour Sauce

Serves 4

Preparation time: 15 minutes
Cooking time: 30 minutes
Calories per serving: 360

Freezing recommended

The four-pronged fork is thought to have been invented in Naples, at the court of King Ferdinand II, to enable spaghetti to be eaten more elegantly!

12 oz (360 g) lean minced pork or turkey
1 garlic clove, crushed
1 oz (30 g) fresh breadcrumbs
7 oz (210 g) spaghetti

For the sauce:
2 teaspoons oil
1 green pepper, de-seeded and sliced
1 red pepper, de-seeded and sliced
1 onion, sliced
1 carrot, cut in thin strips
1 garlic clove, crushed
1 chilli, chopped (optional)
1 teaspoon grated root ginger (optional)
2 tablespoons dark brown sugar
2 tablespoons cornflour
3 tablespoons soy sauce
3 tablespoons tomato purée
4 tablespoons dry sherry
4 tablespoons white wine vinegar
6 tablespoons orange juice
1/4 pint (150 ml) water
salt and freshly ground black pepper

1. Mix the meat with the garlic and breadcrumbs, season well with salt and pepper. Shape into 24 small balls. Sauté the balls in a non-stick pan for about 6–8 minutes until cooked through.
2. Heat the oil in a large frying pan and sauté the peppers, onion, carrot, garlic, chilli and ginger (if using), for 5 minutes. Meanwhile, blend the rest of the sauce ingredients together in a jug. Add the meatballs to the pan and pour in the sauce mixture. Bring to a boil and simmer for 10–15 minutes until the vegetables are just beginning to soften.
3. Meanwhile, cook the spaghetti in a large pan of lightly salted boiling water for 8–10 minutes or until just *al dente*.
4. Drain the spaghetti, divide between 4 warm bowls and serve with the meatballs and sauce on top.

Selections per serving:
2 Carbohydrate; 1/2 Fat; 2 1/2 Protein; 1 Vegetable; 70 Optional Calories

Minced Beef and Pasta Bake

Serves 4

Preparation time: 30 minutes
Cooking time: 30 minutes
Calories per serving: 435

Freezing recommended

1 lb (480 g) lean minced beef
2 onions, chopped
2 carrots, chopped
2 oz (60 g) plain flour
1/2 pint (300 ml) beef stock
3 oz (90 g) macaroni
2 teaspoons margarine
3/4 pint (450 ml) skimmed milk
a pinch of dry mustard
2 oz (60 g) mature Cheddar cheese, grated
salt and freshly ground black pepper

1. Sauté the minced beef in a non-stick saucepan until browned. Drain off the fat and add the onions and carrots. Cook for 5 minutes more until the vegetables begin to soften.
2. Stir in 1/2 oz (15 g) of the flour, and cook gently for 1 minute. Gradually blend in the stock and bring to a boil, stirring constantly, until the liquid thickens. Season with salt and pepper, reduce the heat and simmer for 10 minutes.
3. Meanwhile, cook the macaroni in plenty of lightly salted boiling water for 8–10 minutes or until *al dente*. Preheat the oven to Gas Mark 6/200°C/400°F.
4. Melt the margarine in a medium-size saucepan and stir in the remaining flour. Cook gently for 1 minute and then add the milk gradually. Heat, stirring constantly, until the sauce boils and thickens. Remove from the heat and season with salt, pepper and mustard.
5. Drain the cooked pasta thoroughly. Mix it into the white sauce with half of the grated cheese. Spoon the meat sauce into a 2-pint (1.2 litre) ovenproof dish. Pour the macaroni and sauce on top. Sprinkle with the remaining cheese.
6. Bake for 25–30 minutes until golden brown.

Selections per serving:
1 Carbohydrate; 1/2 Fat; 1/4 Milk; 3 Protein; 1 Vegetable; 60 Optional Calories

Chicken and Broccoli Lasagne

Serves 4

Preparation time: 10–15 minutes
Cooking time: 55 minutes
Calories per serving: 500

Freezing recommended

1 pint (600 ml) skimmed milk
1 bay leaf
a pinch of freshly grated nutmeg
1 onion, sliced finely
8 oz (240 g) fennel, sliced
8 oz (240 g) chicken breast, skinned
8 oz (240 g) (6 sheets) wholewheat lasagne

8 oz (240 g) broccoli, cut in ½-inch (1 cm) florets
1 tablespoon margarine or olive oil
1 oz (30 g) plain flour
3 tablespoons chopped fresh parsley
5 fl oz (150 ml) low-fat natural yogurt
1 egg
3 oz (90 g) Gruyère or Cheddar cheese, grated
2 tomatoes, sliced thickly (optional)
salt and freshly ground black pepper

1. Heat the milk with the bay leaf in a shallow pan and add a generous pinch of grated nutmeg. Add the onion, fennel and chicken and simmer for 12–15 minutes until the vegetables and chicken are just cooked.
2. Meanwhile, parboil the lasagne for 5 minutes or according to pack instructions, steaming the broccoli on the top until it just begins to soften. Drain them both, rinse the lasagne and set aside.
3. Remove the chicken, vegetables and bay leaf from the milk and set aside. Chop the chicken in small pieces. Blend the margarine or oil with the flour and whisk into the hot milk, bringing it to a boil to make a smooth sauce. Cook for a few minutes.
4. Remove from the heat and return the vegetables and chicken to the sauce. Stir in the parsley and season with salt and freshly ground black pepper.
5. Preheat the oven to Gas Mark 5/190°C/375°F. Spoon one third of the sauce into an ovenproof dish. Cover with 2 sheets of lasagne then repeat the layers twice, ending with lasagne on top. Beat the yogurt and egg together and mix in the grated cheese. Pour over the lasagne and sprinkle a little more nutmeg on the top.
6. Bake for 20 minutes, then place the tomato slices on top (if using). Cook for a further 15–20 minutes until golden brown.

Cook's notes:
Serve with baked tomatoes and freshly cooked carrots.
  If you don't like the flavour of fennel, substitute 4 oz (120 g) sliced courgette and 4 oz (120 g) of chopped celery, steamed with the broccoli. Or substitute sliced button mushrooms for half of the broccoli.

Selections per serving:
2 Carbohydrate; ½ Fat; ½ Milk; 2½ Protein; 2 Vegetable; 55 Optional Calories

Turkey Tetrazzini

Serves 4

Preparation time: 20 minutes
Cooking time: 20 minutes
Calories per serving: 550

Freezing recommended

This is an ideal midweek supper recipe to use up the leftover Christmas turkey. Serve it with a crisp green salad.

8 oz (240 g) red, green and
    white tagliatelle or spaghetti
4 teaspoons margarine
1 onion, chopped
4 oz (120 g) button
    mushrooms, sliced finely
1 small green pepper, de-seeded
    and cut in strips
1½ oz (45 g) plain flour
½ pint (300 ml) chicken or
    turkey stock
¼ pint (150 ml) skimmed milk
2 tablespoons dry sherry
14 oz (420 g) cooked turkey,
    cubed
2 oz (60 g) cooked ham, cubed
a pinch of grated nutmeg
2 oz (60 g) mature Cheddar
    cheese, grated
½ oz (15 g) (about 7) plain
    crisps, crumbled
salt and freshly ground black
    pepper

To garnish:
1 tomato, sliced
chopped parsley

1. Cook the pasta in a large saucepan of lightly salted boiling water for 6–8 minutes, or until just tender. Drain thoroughly.
2. Preheat the oven to Gas Mark 5/190°C/375°F.
3. Melt the margarine in a saucepan. Add the onion and cook gently for 5 minutes, until softened. Add the mushrooms and green pepper and cook for 5 minutes more.
4. Sprinkle in the flour and carefully stir it into the vegetables. Gradually add the stock, milk and the sherry. Heat, stirring constantly with a wooden spoon, until the sauce boils and thickens.
5. Remove from the heat and fold in the turkey, ham and pasta. Season with the nutmeg, salt and pepper.
6. Spoon the mixture into an ovenproof gratin dish. Mix together the grated cheese and crisps and sprinkle over the surface. Bake for 20 minutes until golden brown.
7. Garnish with thinly sliced tomato and fresh chopped parsley and serve immediately.

Selections per serving:
2 Carbohydrate; 1 Fat; 4 Protein; 1 Vegetable; 100 Optional Calories

Oriental Hot Duck Salad

Serves 4

Preparation time: 10 minutes
+ 2 hours marinating
Cooking time: 20 minutes
Calories per serving: 300

Freezing not recommended

1 lb 2 oz (540 g) duck breast,
    skinned
1–2 garlic cloves, crushed
2 teaspoons freshly grated root
    ginger
1 small chilli, de-seeded and
    chopped finely
1 tablespoon light soy sauce
2 teaspoons sesame or
    peanut oil
grated zest and juice of 1 lime
6 oz (180 g) pasta shapes
2 medium oranges, peeled,
    segmented and chopped,
    juice reserved
1 bag/bunch watercress or half
    a 2½ oz (75 g) bag of mixed
    salad leaves
salt and freshly ground black
    pepper
2 teaspoons toasted sesame
    seeds, to serve

1. Place the duck breasts into a shallow dish. Mix the garlic, ginger, chilli, soy sauce, sesame oil and lime zest and juice together and spoon over the duck breasts. Cover and leave to marinate in a cool place for about 2 hours.
2. Preheat the grill. Cook the duck breasts, plump side down, for 5 minutes and then turn them and grill for 8–10 minutes more. Use the marinade to baste the duck well during grilling. Set aside until cool enough to handle.
3. Meanwhile, cook the pasta in a large pan of lightly salted boiling water for about 8–10 minutes until just *al dente*.
4. Slice the duck breasts. Drain the pasta and toss with half of the chopped orange segments and all of the reserved juice. Divide the pasta between 4 warm plates and arrange the duck slices on top. Season with salt and pepper and garnish with the watercress, remaining orange segments and the sesame seeds.

Selections per serving:
1½ Carbohydrate; ½ Fat; ½ Fruit; 2½ Protein; 5 Optional Calories

Variation:
Chicken breasts could be used instead of duck breasts.

Pasta with Lambs Liver and Sage

Serves 4

Preparation time: 10 minutes
Cooking time: 25–30 minutes
Calories per serving: 410

Freezing recommended

4 teaspoons vegetable oil
1 onion, sliced
1 red or yellow pepper,
   de-seeded and sliced
1 garlic clove, crushed
12 oz (360 g) lambs liver,
   trimmed and cut in thumb-
   width strips
1/2 oz (15 g) flour
4 oz (120 g) chestnut
   mushrooms, sliced

14 oz (420 g) canned plum
   tomatoes
3 tablespoons red wine
3 tablespoons water
2 teaspoons coarse-grained
   mustard
2 teaspoons chopped fresh sage
   or 1 teaspoon dried sage
a good dash of Worcestershire
   sauce (optional)
6 oz (180 g) pappardelle or
   tagliatelle pasta
salt and freshly ground black
   pepper
sprigs of sage, to garnish

1. Heat 2 teaspoons of the oil in a large non-stick frying pan. Add the onion, pepper and garlic and cook over a medium heat for 4–5 minutes.
2. Meanwhile, place the liver in a plastic bag with the flour and toss it well until the strips are evenly coated. Remove the vegetables from the frying pan with a slotted spoon and set aside. Add the liver and cook over a medium-high heat until sealed on all sides. Stir in the mushrooms and sauté for 1 minute more.
3. Put the vegetables back in the pan and stir in the tomatoes (breaking them up a little), wine, water, mustard, sage and salt and pepper. Bring to a boil, then cover and simmer for 15 minutes until the liver is tender and the sauce is smooth. Add a dash of Worcestershire sauce if you like.
4. Meanwhile, cook the pasta in plenty of lightly salted boiling water for 8–10 minutes or until just *al dente*. Drain well and toss in the remaining 2 teaspoons of oil. Arrange the pasta on hot plates and spoon the liver on top. Garnish with a sprig of fresh sage.

Cook's note:
To add more colour and vegetables to this tasty dish, fold ribbons or thin strips of courgette and carrot into the pasta.

Selections per serving:
1 1/2 Carbohydrate; 1 Fat; 2 1/2 Protein; 2 Vegetable; 20 Optional Calories

Index

Amatriciana sauce **30**
Avocado and orange pasta
   salad **17**

Bakes:
   Leek, bean and caerphilly
      bake **43**
   Minced beef and pasta bake **73**
   Nutty cheese and gnocchi
      bake **37**
   Salmon and pasta bake **60**
Baked Italian fish casserole **59**
Basic white sauce **24**
Beef cannelloni **70**
Bisque, seafood **12**
Blue cheese dressing, with
   pasta **34**
Boston beef and baked bean
   hotpot **70**
Broth, chicken and pasta **12**
Bucatini with tuna and tomato **54**

Cannelloni, beef **70**
Caponata, pasta **20**
Casserole, baked Italian fish **59**
Cauliflower cheese, macaroni
   and **43**
Cheese and tomato pasta
   flan **40**
Cheese and onion sauce, with
   lasagnette **37**
Chicken:
   Chicken and broccoli lasagne **74**
   Chicken and pasta broth **12**
   Chicken liver and mushroom
      medley **65**
   Huntsman chicken **66**
   Spicy chicken and pasta with
      apricots **66**
Cod, chive and parsley sauce, with
   tagliatelle **57**
Courgette and carrot ribbons, with
   pasta **14**
Creamy cheese dressing **24**
Crispy bacon and chives, with
   vermicelli **62**

Dressing, creamy cheese **24**

Flan, cheese and tomato pasta **40**
Four cheeses, with pasta
   quills **45**
Fragrant saffron pasta salad **23**
Fritatta, spaghetti **38**

Gammon and pasta toss **69**
Garlic and mushroom sauce **29**
Gratin, mushroom and
   spinach **40**
Gratin, ratatouille pasta **38**
Greek pasta salad **18**

Haddock and broccoli
   lasagne **50**
Hotpot, Boston beef and baked
   bean **70**
Huntsman chicken **66**

Italian pasta dressing **33**

Lambs liver and sage, with pasta **78**
Lasagne, chicken and
   broccoli **74**
Lasagne, haddock and
   broccoli **50**
Lasagnette with cheese and onion
   sauce **37**
Leek, bean and caerphilly
   bake **43**

Macaroni and cauliflower cheese **43**
Meatballs with spaghetti in sweet
   and sour sauce **73**
Medley, chicken liver and
   mushroom **65**
Melon and prawn salad **48**
Mexican red pepper and tomato
   soup **11**
Minced beef and pasta bake **73**
Minestrone soup **11**
Mushroom and spinach
   gratin **40**

Neapolitan tomato sauce **26**
Nutty cheese and gnocchi
   bake **37**

Oriental hot duck salad **77**

Paprika, pork and pasta **69**
Pasta and basil soup **8**
Pasta bean potage **8**
Pasta and monkfish
   'en papillote' **60**
Pasta caponata **20**
Pasta dressing, Italian **33**
Pasta quills with four
   cheeses **45**
Pasta salad, Greek **18**
Pasta salad Niçoise **53**

Pasta salad with rocket and tomato
   dressing **23**
Pasta with blue cheese dressing **34**
Pasta with lambs liver and sage **78**
Pasta with mushrooms **14**
Pasta with ribbons of courgette and
   carrot **14**
Pasta with sun-dried tomato and
   prawn sauce **54**
Pasta with tuna and black olives **46**
Pepperoni pasta **62**
Pork and pasta paprika **69**
Potage, pasta bean **8**
Provençal stuffed tomatoes **18**

Ratatouille pasta gratin **38**
Red pepper and tomato soup,
   Mexican **11**
Rigatoni with seafood sauce **57**
Roast vegetable salad **20**
Rocket and tomato dressing, pasta
   salad with **23**

Salads:
   Avocado and orange
      salad **17**
   Fragrant saffron pasta
      salad **23**
   Greek pasta salad **18**
   Melon and prawn salad **48**
   Oriental hot duck salad **77**
   Pasta salad Niçoise **53**
   Pasta salad with rocket
      and tomato dressing **23**
   Roast vegetable salad **20**
   Sea shell salad **46**
   Smoked mackerel salad **48**
   Warm spaghetti salad with
      artichokes **17**
Salmon and pasta bake **60**
Sauces:
   Amatriciana sauce **30**
   Basic white sauce **24**
   Creamy cheese dressing **24**
   Garlic and mushroon
      sauce **29**
   Italian pasta dressing **33**
   Neapolitan tomato sauce **26**
   Spinach and ricotta cheese
      sauce **30**
   Sweet red pepper sauce **29**
   Uncooked tomato sauce **26**
   Yogurt and herb sauce **33**

Sausage, with tomato pasta **65**
Sea shell salad **46**
Seafood sauce, with rigatoni **57**
Seafood bisque **12**
Smoked salmon and asparagus,
   with tagliatelle **59**
Smoked mackerel salad **48**
Soups:
   Chicken and pasta broth **12**
   Mexican red pepper and tomato
      soup **11**
   Minestrone soup **11**
   Pasta and basil soup **8**
   Pasta bean potage **8**
   Seafood bisque **12**
Spaghetti:
   Meatballs with spaghetti in
      sweet and sour sauce **73**
   Spaghetti carbonara **34**
   Spaghetti fritatta **38**
   Spaghetti marinara **53**
   Warm spaghetti salad with
      artichokes **17**
Spicy chicken and pasta with
   apricots **66**
Spinach and ricotta cheese sauce **30**
Stuffed tomatoes, Provençal **18**
Sun-dried tomato and prawn sauce,
   with pasta **54**
Sweet red pepper sauce **29**

Tagliatelle with cod, chive and
   parsley sauce **57**
Tagliatelle with smoked salmon and
   asparagus **59**
Tomato sauce, uncooked **26**
Tomato pasta with sausage **65**
Tomato sauce, Neapolitan **26**
Tuna and tomato, with
   bucatini **54**
Tuna and black olives, with
   pasta **46**
Turkey tetrazzini **77**

Uncooked tomato sauce **26**

Vermicelli with crispy bacon and
   chives **62**

Warm spaghetti salad with
   artichokes **17**
White sauce, basic **24**

Yogurt and herb sauce **33**